A Mediaeval Prince of Wales

THE LIFE OF GRUFFUDD AP CYNAN

A MEDIAEVAL PRINCE OF WALES:
THE LIFE OF GRUFFUDD AP CYNAN.

D. SIMON EVANS.

ISBN 0947992472

The author wishes to acknowledge gratefully the assistance received from the Leverhulme Trust in the preparation of this work.

CENTRE FOR RESEARCH AND SCHOLARSHIP
ST. DAVID'S UNIVERSITY COLLEGE
LAMPETER, DYFED.

For the Principal
The Rt. Hon. the Lord Morris of Castle Morris
A scholar, and a friend of scholars.

CONTENTS

INTRODUCTION

While there is no evidence that Gruffudd ap Cynan himself possessed qualities which marked him off from other leaders, the circumstances of his life in so far as they can be known, are certainly significant and noteworthy. His life (from c. 1055 to 1137) covers an important period in both Welsh and English history. The Normans came to England and later to Wales, and their advent resulted in changes and developments which permanently affected life and culture in these lands.

The twelfth century was certainly a time of change, when new and penetrating influences were at work. The Crusades brought people into contact and conflict with parts and people hitherto little known. There was generally more travel in all directions; more intercourse, more trade, the introduction of newer methods and techniques. It was the time which witnessed the growth of universities and the revival of learning.

In Wales there is clear evidence of a renaissance in many facets of life, some of it (but not all) attributable to movements from outside. There must have been interest in the study and practice of law. There was reform in church organisation; churches were re-dedicated doubtless to the detriment of the cult of many Celtic saints, who, however, seemed at this time to acquire a new lease of life from both Welsh and Norman patrons. Many lives of saints were produced during the century, all written in Latin, a language widely used in Wales, in the production of law books and ecclesiastical works such as the Book of Llandaff, of historical works such as 'The History of the Kings of Britain' by Geoffrey of Monmouth (?c.1136), of chronicles such as the Chronicles of the Princes and various other works. In the twelfth century there was an unmistakable flowering of the poetic craft, as is evidenced by the poetry of the Gogynfeirdd, or the Poets of the Princes. One of the earliest of these was Meilyr Brydydd, who composed an elegy to Gruffudd ap Cynan. This poem is, of course, the work of an admirer, whose privilege and duty it was to declare and declaim unqualified praise. In this respect he is to be compared with the author of the Life, which was likewise composed at some date after the prince's death. Neither the elegy nor the life presents an objective assessment of the prince, but the two offer the most comprehensive evidence of him we possess. Some other sources are available, not all of them necessarily complimentary or biased in his favour. The most important among them is Brut y Tywysogion, which seeks to present a history of Welsh princes from 682 to 1282 (and later in some texts). Gruffudd is often referred to, more especially in the twelfth century, when the annals become fuller and there is more news to record. Mention may be made also of other works, which, although they have little to say about Gruffudd himself, provide useful information regarding events and circumstances in his time. We have the Lives of Saints, more especially that of Gwynllyw, The Book of Llandaff, concerned with the interests of the newly formed diocese, and the writings of various authors connected with Wales, such as Walter Map and Gerald the Welshman. From the poetry of the period, including vaticinatory verse, we can glean some information. Outside Wales there are some important Norman and English authors, such as Ordericus Vitalis, Florence of Worcester, William of Malmesbury and others, the *Anglo-Saxon Chronicle* and *Domesday Book*. Irish and Scandinavian sources may also be consulted.

Gruffudd was the first in a line of princes which survived (indeed, at times, flourished) as rulers of Gwynedd up till the death of the last prince in 1282. His reign was regarded as ushering in a new era in literature, religion, learning and politics. The princes of Gwynedd after him sought to promote the concept of a Welsh feudal state in which other leaders in the principality owed allegiance and homage to the ruler of Gwynedd as Prince of Wales, rather than to the English crown, an outlook and attitude which seems reflected in the *Historia*.

Let us now follow his career as it is revealed to us in the sources mentioned above, more especially here in his Life. First we have a detailed description of his pedigree, where it is shown how he was related to Irish, Scandinavian and Norman kings and leaders. He also had a place in the line of Welsh kings from the very earliest period. His father Cynan was son of Iago, ruler of Gwynedd until he was slain in 1039, but Cynan did not succeed his father. He fled to Ireland, or so it appears. Gruffudd was born there (c.1055) and spent his youth there. It is, of course, impossible to disprove this, although one must have some reservations about it. In Irish chronicles there are many references to Welsh leaders, to Llywelyn ap Seisyll, Iago (Gruffudd's grandfather), Gruffudd ap Llywelyn, Rhys ap Tewdwr, Llywelyn ap Gruffudd and his brother Dafydd. But some have es-

11

caped mention and among them Gruffudd ap Cynan, which seems surprising for one reputed to have been born and bred in Dublin. While it would be rash to jump to conclusions, one is nevertheless justified in questioning some (if not all) of Gruffudd's supposed Irish connections. One theory which may be mentioned is that these could have been devised in order to explain a missing link in his claim to the kingdom of Gwynedd. Although the *Historia* describes his father Cynan as king of Gwynedd, he had never held that position, and an explanation is called for. The Brut sometimes refers to Gruffudd as *wyr Iago* 'grandson of Iago,' and the obscurity surrounding the movements of Cynan could be explained by reference to the circumstance of his having been obliged to seek refuge in Ireland, where he met and married a girl of mixed Irish and Scandinavian stock, a girl of renown who could be identified but who was never at any time linked with the name of Cynan in any other source. Cynan would thus have fled to Ireland where conveniently he died young. Such a story, if that is what it is, would not require much convincing. After all, there was a fairly long tradition of leaders from Wales crossing to Ireland in search of refuge and help. Geoffrey of Monmouth tells us that Pasgen went there and later Cadwallon, in the seventh century, fleeing from Edwin of Northumbria. According to the *Annals of Ulster*, Rhodri Mawr fled there from the Danes in 877. It happened more than once during our own period according to the Brut. In the *Historia* it is said that Gruffudd ap Cynan himself retreated to Ireland five times at least. Others also went there: Rhys ap Tewdwr in 1088, Cadwgan ap Bleddyn (with Gruffudd ap Cynan) in 1098, Hywel ab Ithel in 1099, Owain ap Cadwgan

12

in 1109, and again in 1110, he and Madog ap Rhiddid, Maelgwn ab Owain Gwynedd in 1173.

The relationship between Wales and Ireland is one of the knotty problems of early Welsh history during the first milennium of the Christian era. It would be patently absurd and impossible to try and disentangle it here, where we can only refer to it and stress its importance as an area of study which impinges upon the life and movements of Gruffudd ap Cynan, especially in his earlier years. We shall now resume our study of his life during those early years, as it is described to us.

Gruffudd is said to have been born and reared in Dublin. His mother spoke to him of the patrimony to which he was entitled in Gwynedd, and eventually (in 1075) he set sail for Wales and reached the harbour of Abermenai. Gwynedd, which was his kingdom by right, was being ruled by usurpers, namely Trahaearn son of Caradog from Arwystli and Cynwrig son of Rhiwallon from Powys. We have next an account of his efforts to win back his kingdom, by far the longest section in the book; it covers in all a period of twenty-five years, from 1075 to 1100. With the help of men from Gwynedd and also of Robert, a Norman baron from Rhuddlan, he succeeds in subduing Gwynedd in 1075. He defeated Trahaearn and his men in Gwaed-erw in the cantref of Meirionnydd. Then to our surprise we find him attacking the Norman baron Robert, an incident which may well have been misplaced here. Further there is mention of discontent among his followers, the Welsh and the soldiers from Ireland, a situation of which Trahaearn took full advantage, and Gruffudd was defeated in a bloody battle in Bron-yr-erw, near

Clynnog Fawr. He fled to Wexford, then returned to Abermenai where he met with little success. His men went back to their country and took him with them, while the Normans and the men of Powys came to Gwynedd where they plundered and caused much damage. Thus for the first time in the life of Gruffudd we find success followed by reverse, reverse caused by treachery. It was to happen again.

Then Gruffudd came with a fleet of Scandinavians, Irish and Welsh from Waterford, and landed in Porth Clais, close to St. David's. At St. David's he met Rhys ap Tewdwr, king of Deheubarth, in retreat before his enemies. They joined forces and some distance to the north together fought the battle of Mynydd Carn, a battle recorded in poetry and in the Brut under 1081. Here Gruffudd defeated his enemies and went on to Arwystli and Powys but once more success was short-lived, because of treachery by one of his men. Gruffudd was put in prison, where he remained for twelve (or sixteen) years. Ordericus Vitalis also refers to his capture (by Robert of Rhuddlan), but one must feel uneasy about so long an imprisonment. We saw that his Irish birth and upbringing could be explained as an attempt to conceal a weakness in his claim to rule in Gwynedd. One is likewise tempted to ask whether the story of his long imprisonment had a similar purpose. There is evidence from other sources that during this period Gruffudd lived the life of a pirate, a role which would hardly enhance his claim to govern, while putting him in prison for a reasonable period of time would conveniently remove him from the scene. This must remain a suggestion, which may or may not be substantiated, but it needs to be said that this episode both in general outline and in detail is not altogether convincing.

He eventually escaped from prison, and then moved from place to place in the South, in Ardudwy and in Gwynedd where he caused much damage and was not regarded with favour. More than once he sailed to Ireland and back. He also sought the help of his ally, Godfrey king of the Isles. He went to Llŷn and there seems to have had a more encouraging response from the men of Gwynedd. This must have been in 1094, when the Welsh had had their fill of Norman oppression and were ready for revolt. We are here told that the men of Llŷn, Eifionydd, Ardudwy, Arfon, Rhos and Dyffryn Clwyd flocked to Gruffudd. With a large force he attacked a castle in Anglesey and destroyed it. He proceeded to destroy other castles in Gwynedd and to take possession of the land; then there was peace in Gwynedd for two years.

Gruffudd's wife was Angharad, daughter of Owain ab Edwin. By her he had three sons, Cadwallon, Owain and Cadwaladr, and five daughters, Gwenllian, Rhainillt, Susanna and Annest; as well as children by other women.

There are accounts of two expeditions to Wales by William Rufus, in 1095 and 1097, but the *Historia* mentions only one, directed against Gwynedd. This was singularly unsuccessful, and brought the king no gain except for one cow (*namen vn vuch*). We are next told of an expedition (in 1098) against Gwynedd and Powys by the two Norman earls, the two Hughs, earls of Chester and Shrewsbury. Gruffudd and his allies retreated to Anglesey, and were betrayed by a

15

band of mercenaries from Ireland who had come to help them. Gruffudd and his somewhat fickle son-in-law, Cadwgan ap Bleddyn, fled to Ireland, leaving their people to the will of God and His protection, which proved of little avail to them against the crude and cruel ravaging of the Normans. Suddenly and unexpectedly there appeared off the coast of Anglesey a fleet under Magnus, king of Norway. This soon became involved in a savage skirmish with the Normans in which Hugh, earl of Shrewsbury, was killed and the Normans defeated. Magnus then left, to the great relief of the Normans, and Hugh, earl of Chester, moved the men of Gwynedd and their effects to the cantref of Rhos, for fear of the arrival of Gruffudd at any time. Gruffudd returned from Ireland, to find his land desolate and his people transferred to another place. He then sent emissaries to Hugh, and made peace with him, whereby he obtained three townships in that cantref.

We next learn of a visit by him to Henry, king of England, as a result of which he obtained the cantrefs of Llŷn and Eifionydd, Ardudwy and Arllechwedd. It appears that by means of diplomacy Gruffudd eventually succeeded in achieving what he had failed to gain through warfare. From then on indubitable success attended his endeavours, and his people flocked back to Gwynedd from exile in various parts. Such success, however, aroused the suspicion of the king, who came to Wales with the intention of destroying Gruffudd and his territory. These expeditions occurred in 1114 and 1121, and are recorded in the Brut. Any confusion or distress they may have caused, however, was short-lived, and for the remainder of his time Gruffudd seems to have lived a life of peace and prosperity. He established a good relationship with his neighbours, in England, Ireland and the Isles, and he himself won fame and renown both far and near. In Gwynedd wealth increased and churches were built everywhere. Woods were planted, as were orchards and gardens. He ruled his people with an iron rod and set his sons over border areas to defend them against foreign peoples. The smaller kings sought his court and his protection whenever they were harassed by such peoples.

When Gruffudd grew old and lost the sight of his eyes, he retired to lead a godly life and completely forsook his worldly power. He decided to distribute his wealth, some of which he gave to churches in Ireland, some to St. David's and border areas such as Chester and Shrewsbury, and some to churches in north Wales, such as Bangor and Meifod. At his death-bed there were present David, bishop of Bangor, Symeon the archdeacon, the prior of the Chester monastery (who is not named), as well as priests and scholars anointing his body. Also present were his children and his wife Angharad, to whom he gave half his possessions, two land-portions and the harbour of Abermenai (probably a reference to ferry charges). His death was followed by much grief and mourning among Welsh, Irish and the people of the Isles. He was eighty-two years of age when he died, and was buried in a vault on the left side of the high altar in the church at Bangor.

Why was this Life written, and when? It was originally composed in Latin, doubtless by an ecclesiastic and a diplomat, who must have been close to the centre of power in Gwynedd, possibly David who was archdeacon in Bangor in the sixties of the twelfth century and possibly a son of Simeon, who was also archdeacon and apparently present at Gruffudd's deathbed. It is clear that it had a political motive and was intended to enhance the power and prestige of Gwynedd under Gruffudd's son, Owain. As a historical document its value must remain suspect. Events which do not redound to the glory of Gruffudd are studiously shunned, as it was clearly the author's intention to portray him solely as a man of prowess, honour and diplomatic acumen, whose progress was nevertheless bedevilled by constant ill-luck and treachery. Both accounted for set-backs to progress in the case of other great men also; and instances are cited.

It was then a piece of propaganda, a manifesto, designed to bolster the claims of Gwynedd and was composed during the reign of Gruffudd's son Owain. It is made clear at the beginning that Gruffudd belonged to the same stock as the kings of neighbouring peoples, Normans, Scandinavians, Irish, in addition to being firmly and securely in the line of the old Welsh kings from the very earliest period, going back to the pristine glory of Adam.

Are there times in the life of Owain which would have been conducive to the production of such a work? Let us first look at the final period of his life, 1162-70. His mother Angharad died in 1162, and the Brut tells us that this caused her son no little sorrow. The story of the life is described as 'old' (hen) when it was recounted. In 1165 the king Henry II came on an expedition to

Wales, an expedition successfully resisted by Gruffudd who mustered the forces of Gwynedd at Corwen in Edeyrnion, where he was joined by other Welsh princes. The *Historia* may well have been composed to set the seal on this military and diplomatic supremacy, when the various parts of Wales seem to have been united under his leadership. This was his finest hour.

Another time which may be considered is 1157, when Henry II, who had been on the throne since 1154, came to Wales to control and subdue the unruly Welsh, and Owain in particular. Although Owain was not defeated, he was obliged to submit and pay homage, as his father had done after the expedition of Henry I in 1114. As a result he lost territories and was facing a critical situation. We can detect some suggestive echoes of this in the *Historia*. The prince of Powys and Arwystli, and even his own brother Cadwaladr were on the king's side. Towards the south Ceredigion was now part of Deheubarth, and Rhys ap Gruffudd's endeavours were meeting with success. Indeed, the situation of 1157 seems reflected by some of the features in the *Historia*. There is furthermore the author's attitude towards the leaders of Powys and Deheubarth, and the emphasis on Gruffudd's superiority over all his opponents, including at times the king of England. A work such as this would help the cause of Gwynedd and its prince at a sensitive time of crisis and anguish, such as was experienced in 1157.

We may go to an earlier period still in the life of Owain Gwynedd. The work could have been composed fairly soon after the death of Gruffudd. Let us look at the political situation. For years before Gruffudd's death, his sons Owain and Cadwaladr had been engaged in warfare against Powys, and the hostility towards Powys evidenced in the *Historia* may reflect an earlier as well as a later situation. Similarly the attitude towards Rhys ap Tewdwr (d. 1093) and Deheubarth. Gruffudd ap Rhys and the sons of Gruffudd ap Cynan were allies in 1136, and Owain Gwynedd's policy throughout his reign was to try and secure peace and co-operation with Deheubarth, a policy not always successful. We hear of conflict in the earlier period, as in 1151-2 when the sons of Gruffudd ap Rhys seized Ceredigion from Cadwaladr and Owain's son Hywel. Such confrontation and conflict may explain the desire of the *Historia* to establish the superiority of Gruffudd over Rhys ap Tewdwr. Then there is the vexed question of the authority of Canterbury. Too much weight should not perhaps be given to the description of Mynyw as an *archescopty* 'archbishop's house,' but one cannot ignore the support given by Owain and Cadwaladr to Bishop Bernard's campaign for metropolitan status for St. David's between 1139 and 1143. It may well be that archdeacon Simeon played an important part in the support given to St. David's by the princes of Gwynedd, and it is significant that in 1147/8 bishop Bernard requested him to give evidence before the Pope.

All three periods are possible, but on balance it appears that the final period of Owain's reign, in the sixties, is the most probable.

The original Latin text of the *Historia* has not been preserved, and we only have the Welsh version, which seems to be a very close translation of the original. This version is contained (in an incomplete copy) in only one early text, namely that of Peniarth MS 17, which may be dated to about the middle of the thirteenth century. It would be tedious here to describe in detail this MS and its relation to other later MSS of the text. Suffice it to say that in the Welsh edition I have provided a description of the textual history of the *Historia* down to the minutest detail, in a study which occupied many weary months and years. The results of that study are given here in bare outline. Between 1200 and 1550 it appears that very few copies were made. The only early surviving copy is that of Peniarth 17, and there is (indirect) evidence for only one other text, which can be no earlier than the fourteenth century; indeed it could be much later. It is not possible for us to determine on what text it was based, whether it was Peniarth 17 or some other text. What can with certainty be established is that all the later texts, some twelve in all, are derived from it. These later texts, which appear from the middle of the sixteenth century on, provide evidence of renewed interest in the *Historia* in that century and later by men of nobility and learning. There was also renewed interest at this time generally in history and genealogy, and one is impressed by the many references at this time to Gruffudd ap Cynan. He was regarded as the promoter of enterprising movements and the statute drawn up to regulate the activities of the bards in the sixteenth century was named after him. We have further evidence of the popularity of the *Historia* in the fact that a Latin translation of it was produced sometime during the third quarter of the sixteenth century, some ten copies of which have survived.

The two earliest texts among the later Welsh copies are found in British Library MS Cotton Vitelius Cix, and Peniarth 267 copied by John Jones of Gellilyfdy when he was a prisoner in the Fleet in London (1635-41). The text published here is that of Peniarth 17 as much of it as has survived; the remainder being supplied from Peniarth 267. For a full account of the manuscript sources, cf. *HGK* cclvii-cclxxxix.

HISTORIA GRUFFUD VAB KENAN

[Peniarth 17. 1-16, 267. 373-86]

Eman e dechreu historia hen
Gruffud vab Kenan vab Yago.

[Ei eni]
En dydyeu Edward, vrenhin Lloegyr a Therdelach,
vrenhin Ywerdon e ganet Gruffud vrenhin Gwyned
en Ywerdon, en dinas Dulyn; ac yg kymvt
Colomcell y magwyt, y lle a elwir yg Gwydelec
Svrth Colomcell. A tri milltir yv henne y urth y
lle yd oed y vam a'e vamvaeth.

[Ei rieni]
Y dat oed Kenan, vrenhin Gvyned, a'e vam oed
Ragnell verch Avloed, vrenhin dinas Dulyn a
phymet rann Ywerdon. Ac urth henne, bonhedicaf
gur oed y Gruffud hvnnv o vrenhinyaul genedel a
llinyoed goruchel, megys y tysta ac [y traeth]a
bonhed y reeni.

[Ei ach o du ei dad]
Canys mab oed Gruffudd y Gynan vrenhin,m. Yago,
m. Idwal, m. Elissed, m. Meuryc, m. Anaraut, m.
Rodri,m.Etill, verch Kenan o gastell Dindaethue,m.
Idwaldere, m. Catwalader Vendigeit, m. Catwallaun,
m. Catvan, m. Yago, m. Beli, m. Run, m. Maelgun,
m. Catwallavn Llauhir, m. Einnyavn Yrth, m.
Cuneda vrenhin, m. Edern, m. Padern Peisrud, m.
Tagit, m. Yago, m. Guidauc, m. Kein, m. Gorgein,
m. Doli, m. Gurdoli, m. Dwuyn, m. Gorduvyn, m.
Anwerit, m. Onnet, m. Diuwng, m. Brychwein, m.
Ewein, m. Auallach, m. Aflech, m. Beli Maur.
    Rodri Maur, m. Mervyn Vrych, m. Guryat, m.
Elidir, m. Sandef, m. Alcwn, m. Tagit, m. Gveir,

m. Dwc, m. Llewarch Hen, m. Elidir Lledanwyn, m. Meirchyaun Gul, m. Gorwst Ledlumm, m. Keneu, m. Coel Godebauc, m. Tecvan Gloff, m. Deheweint, m. Vrban, m. Grad, m. Riuedel, m. Rideyrn, m. Euteyrn, m. Eudygant, m. Eudos, m. Eudolen, m. Avallach, m. Aflech, m. Beli Mavr, m. Manogan, m. Eneit, m. Kerwyt, m. Krydon, m. Dyvynarth, m. Prydein, m. Aet Maur, m. Antonius, m. Seiryoel, m. Gurust, m. Riwallaun, m. Regat, uerch Lyr, m. Rud, m. Bleidud, m. Lliwelyt, m. Brutus Ysgwyt Ir, m. Membyr, m. Madauc, m. Llocrinus, m. Brut tywyssauc o Ruvein, m. Siluius, m. Ascanius, m. Eneas Ysgwyt Wyn, m. Anchises, m. Capis, m. Assaracus, m. Trois, m. Herictonius, m. Dardanus, m. Iupiter, m. Sadurn, m. Celius, m. Cretus, m. Ciprius, m. Iauan, m. Iaphet, m. Noe Hen, m. Lamech, m. Mathussalem, m. Enoc, m. Iaret, m. Malaleel, m. Cainan, m. Enos, m. Seth, m. Adaf, m. Duw.

[Ei ach o du ei fam]
[2] Bonhed Gruffud o barth y vam: Gruffud vrenhin, m. Ragnell, verch Avloed, vrenhin dinas Dulyn a phymhet ran Ywerdon ac enys Vanav, a hanoed gynt o deyrnas Prydein. A brenhin oed ar lawer o enyssed ereill, Denmarc, a Galwei, a Renneu, a Mon, a Gvyned, en e lle y gwnaeth Avloed castell cadarn a'e dom a'e fos etwa en amlwc, ac a elwit castell Avloed vrenhin; yg Kymraec, hagen, y gelwir Bon y Dom. Avloed enteu oed vab y Sutric vrenhin, m. Avloed, vrenhin Cuaran, m. Sutric, m. Avloed vrenhin, m. Harfagyr vrenhin, m. brenhin Denmarc.

[Harald Harfagyr a'i frodyr]
A bit honneit bot Harald Harfagyr a'e deu vroder yn veibeon y vrenhin Llychlyn. Ac Alyn y

vravt oed vrenhin kyssygredicaf ac enwocaf ymphlith holl Denmarc, ac a ladaud Thur tywyssauc ym brvyder. A thra ytoed hvnnv en e yspeillyav ac en tynnv torch vaur o eur y am y uwnvgyl, mal y gnotaei y brenhined a'r bonhedigyon y arwein gynt, y glynws y dwylav urth y dorch a'e glinyeu urth y groth. A hvnnv vu y gwyrth kentaf a wnaeth Duw yrdav. Ac o henne allan y kymerassant yr holl Daenysseit evo yn sant, ac y hanrydedassant o'r dyd hvnnv allan. A llawer o egluysseu a adeilwt en y enw ac en e anryded ef en Denmarc, a'r mordwywyr a alwant arnav en wahanredaul, ac a aberthant idav ac a offrymant idav llawer o rodyon pan beryclont en e mor. E tywyssauc a'e lladaud enteu a elwit o'r gueithret hvnnv allan Thurkiaul, am lad ohonav y brenhin guiryon.

A bit honneit ry gerdet ar vor o dri broder y racdywededic hvnnv y gyrchu miluryaeth gan vrenhinyaul lynghes. Ac en e diwed wynt a doethant y gyt hyt en Ywerdon. Harald Harfagyr eissyoes a gerdassei kyn no henne a dirvaur lu ganthav, ac a damgylchynus holl Ywerdon gan greulonder, a llad y chivdaut ac eu fo, a'e goresgyn ar hyt ac ar llet. Ac yd adeilws enteu dinas Dulyn a llawer o dinassoed ereill a chestyll a lleoed cadarn, ac y velly cadarnhau a guastatau y deyrnas en e chylch o gylch. Ac vn o'e vroder a ossodes yn vn o'r dinassoed a adeilassei, er honn a elwit yn eu hyeith hwy Porthlarg; a'e etived enteu a vuant vrenhined y dinas hvnnv er henne hyt hediv. Harald eissyoes a wledychus tros wynep Ywerdon ac enyssed Denmarc, y rei ysyd en e mor kyuarystlys a [3] thal enys Prydein, megys y mae enyssed Ciclade y rung mor Tyren a Denmarc.

E trydyd braut enteu, nyt amgen Rodulf, a

gerdus a'e lynges y Freinc, ac eno y gvastataus ac y gorvu ar y Freinc o emlad, ac e goresgynnvs rann vaur o Freinc a elwir er aur hon Nordmandi, canys gvyr Nordwei a'e presswyllya; sef yu y rei henne kenedel o Lychlyn. A'r daear honno a rannwt en deudec rann, herwyd y barwnyeit a'r tywyssogyon a doethant en gentaf y'r ran o Freinc a elwir Brytaen, neu Lydav. Wynt a adeilassant eno dinassoed llawer: Rodum, nyt amgen y gan Rodulf vrenhin y hadeilyauder, a enwyt megys Ruvein y gan Romulus, a Remys y gan Remo; a llawer o dinassoed ereill a chestyll a lleoed cadarn a oruc. O hvnnv yd henynt brenhined Nordmann-yeit a oresgynnassant Loegyr o vrwyder, nyt amgen Guilim vrenhin a'e deu vab enteu, y rei a doethant en e le, Guilim Gledyf Hir a Henri ac Ystyphan y nei, y rei a oedent gytoeswyr y Gruffud vrenhin.

Ac y vegys henne y bu vonhed Gruffudd vrenhin o barth y vam, herwyd tat y vam.

[Ei ach o du ei henfam]

Eilweith o barthret y henvam, nyt amgen mam y vam, Gruffud vrenhin oed vab y Ragnell, merch Vaylcorcre, verch Dunlug, m. Tethel, vrenhin Laine, pymhet ran Ywerdon. Slani, hagen, mam Avloed vrenhin, oed verch y Vrien, brenhin Muen, dwy rann o Ywerdon. Ac odena Gurmlach oed vam Sutric vrenhin; merch oed honno y Vwrchath, vrenhin Laine. Ac y hvnnw y bu tri meib clotvaur, nyt amgen, Dunchath, vrenhin Muen, a Sutric, vrenhin dinas Dulyn, a Moelchelen, vrenhin Midif. Maelmorda, eissyoes, oed vab y'r vrenhines honno o Vwrchath, brenhin Laine.

Y Gruffudd vrenhin yd oed deu vroder vnvam, brenhined Wltw; nyt amgen Ranalld, m. Mathgauyn, yr hvnn a enillws dwy rann o Ywerdon ym pytheunos a mis o'e dewred. Llemhidyd anryved oed; nyt oed o'r holl Wydyl a allei na gurthuynebu na cheffylybu idav en y neit. Y varch enteu oed odidauc yn amravaellyon gampeu o vuander; Islimach oed y enw: kemeint oed eu neit, ef a'e varch. Tebycaf oed y Cinnar, march Achelarw, ac y Bucefal, march Alexander amperauder. Y braut arall y Gruffud oed Ethumachgavyn, brenhin Ultw.

[Ei ach 'herwyd Duw']

Can deryw riuaw boned a charant Gruffud vrenhin herwyd byt, riuwn weithyon y vonhed herwyd Duw; herwyd y dyweit tat sant ac o'e vonhed [4] ef ac o vonhed pob den yn exponyat a wnaeth ar y wers honn o'r Sallwyr: 'Chui yu y dwyweu a meibeon y goruchelaf yu pawb.' Urth henne Gruffud oed vab y Gynan, m. Adaf, m. Duw.

[Darogan Myrddin]

Vrth henne, en y bo canmoledic Gruffud vrenhin o vonhed bydaul ac vn dwywaul, kerdwn weitheon ar darogan Merdin, vard y Brytanyeit, ohonav. Ef a'e daroganvs Merdin ef ynni val hynn:

> Llyminauc lletfer a daroganer,
> Anaeth diarvor dygosel.
> Llegrur y enw, llycraut llawer.

Sef yu henne en Lladin: *'Saltus ferinus praesagitur uenturus de mari insidiaturus cuius nomen corruptor, quia multos corrumpet.'*

O garedicaf vrodyr Kemry, coffaadwy yavn yu Gruffud vrenhin, er hvnn a ganmawl y uonhed bydaul a darogan Merdin val hynn. A chanys deryv henne, bryssyvn y'v briodolyon weithredoed, herwyd yd edewit gennym trwy hen gyvarwydyt. A Christ a vo audur a chynhelwr ynn y henne, ac nyt Diana nac Apollo.

[Ei ieuenctid]

Wrth henne, pan ytoed Gruffud etwa en vab da y deuodeu a drythyll y vagyat, ac yn esgynnv ar vlwydyned y yeuengtit en ty e vam, ac en troi ymplith y chenedel, ymplith henne y managei y vamm idav beunyd pwy a pha ryv wr oed y dat, a pha dref tat oed idav, a pha ryv vrenhinyaeth, a pha ryw dreiswyr a oed en e phressvyllyav. A phan gigleu enteu henne, gorthrum y kemyrth a thrist vu llawer o dydyeu. Ac urth henne y kerdus enteu y lys Mvrchath vrenhin, a chvynav urthav ef en benhaf, ac urth vrenhined Ywerdon y lleill, bot estravn genedloed en argluydi ar y dadaul deyrnas, ac adolwyn udunt yn ysmalha rodi canorthuy idav y geissyav tref y dat. A thruanu urthav a orugant, ac adav canorthuy idav pan delei amser. A phan gigleu er atep, llawen vu, a dioluch henne y Duw ac udunt wynteu.

[Hwylio i Wynedd]

En y lle esgynnv llong a oruc, a dyrchavael hwyllyeu y'r gvynt, a cherdet mor parth a Chemry, a chaffael porth Abermenei. Ac ena yd oedent en argluydiau yn enwir ac en erbyn dylyet Trahaearn vab Caradauc a Chenwric vab Riwallavn, brenhinyn o Bowys, ar holl Wyned, a'e rannv y rygthunt ry daroed udunt.

Ac ena yd anvones Gruffud gennadeu ar wyr Mon ac Arvon, a thri meib Merwyd o Leyn, Asser a Meiryavn a Gugavn, a guyrda ereill, y erchi [5] udunt dyuot ar vrys y gyfruch ac ef. Ac hep ohir wynteu a doethant, a chyvarch guell idav, a dywedut urthav: 'O damunet ry doethost.' Ena yd adolygus enteu o'e holl enni udunt hwy y ganorthuyav y gaffael tref y dat, canys ef oed eu

28

hargluyd priodaur, a gurthlad y gyt ac ef yn wychyr o arveu eu ampriodoryon argluydi dyuot o le arall.

Ac en e bei tervynedic y kyfruch, a gvahanedic y kyngor, y kerdus drachevyn y weilgi parth a chastell Rudlan hyt ar Robert Rudlan, barwn enwavc, dewr, o gedernyt, nei y Hu yarll Caer, a'e wediav a oruc am ganorthuy en erbyn y elynyon a oedent ar dref y dat. A phan gigleu enteu puy oed ef, ac y ba beth ry dothoed, a pha arch oed er eidav, ef a edewis bot en ganorthuywr idav.

[Darogan Tangwystl]

Ac en henne e doeth gureic brud, Tangwystyl y henw, y gares e hun, gureic Lewarch Olbwch, y gyvarch gwell y Gruffud y char, ac y darogan y uot en vrenhin raclaw, a rodi idav y krys meinhaf a goreu, a pheis wedy y gvneithur o ysgin Gruffud vrenhin, m. Llewelyn vrenhin, m. Seissill: canys Llewarch y gur hitheu oed wahanredolaf guas ystavell a thrysoryer y Gruffud, m. Llewelyn.

[Goresgyn Gwynedd]

Odena Gruffud a esgynnws y long, ac a emchuelus o'e reidwyf hyt yn Abermenei.

Odena yd anvones emladwyr meibeon Merwyd, a oedent yg Kelynnavc ar nodva rac ouyn gwyr Powys a oed yn eu gogyuadau, a bonhedigyon ereill oc eu kenedel, a thri ugeinwyr etholedigyon o Degeingyl o gyuoeth y Robert a enwyt uchot, a phetwar ugeinwyr o enys Von, hyt yg cantref Lleyn y emlad a Chenwric vrenhinyn, eu treisswr. Odena y kerdassant wynteu en ystrywus, ac y doethant am y benn en dirybud, ac y lladassant ef a llawer o'e wyr.

Ac ena yd oed Gruffud en Abermenei, nyt amgen

29

y borthloed a dywetpuyt uchot, en arhos pa dynghetven a damweinnyei udunt. Ac ena y kerdus o'r blaen ar vrys guryanc o Arvon, Einnyavn oed y enw, y vynegi chuedyl hyrwyd en gentaf, nyt amgen ry lad y oresgynnvr, ac erchi en goeluein enwedic gureic dec, Delat oed y henw, gordderch y Vledyn vrenhin kyn no henne: megys y dothoed gynt [6] nebun wryanc, mab y wr o Amalech, ar y redec ar Dauid hyt en Philistim o'r vrwyder ry vuassei y menyd Gelboe, a theyrn-wyalen a breichrwy Saul vrenhin ganthav: a'r breichrwy a rodes Dauyd idav enteu en llawen en e goelvein am y chuedel llewenyd.

Odena y doethant en ol gan vudugolyaeth e niuer a anvonessit e'r kyrch. Ac en e lle yd annogassant wynteu idav ef kerdet racdav o'r coel da hvnnv, y oreskyn Mon ac Arvon a Lleyn a'r cantreuoed kyffinyd y Loegyr, a chemryt guryogaeth y gan eu guerin. A cherdet y velly a gogylchynu holl Wyned, y wir dref tat ef, a rodassei Duw en eu llaw hwy o'e drugared Ef.

Ac en e bei wneithuryedic y petheu henne, oc eu hannoc wy y dyduc dirvaur lv parth a chantref Meiryonnyd, en e lle yd oed Trahaearn en y erbyn, y oresgynnvr ef y llall. A brwyder a vu y ryngthunt yg glynn kyving, y lle a elwir yg Kymraec Gvaet Erw, neu y Tir Gvaetlyt, o achaus y vrwyder a vu ena. A Duw a rodes budugolyaeth o'e elynyon en e dyd hvnnv, a llawer o vilyoed a digvydassant o barth Trahaearn; a breid y diengis enteu en gvynvanus, ac ychydic gyt ac ef, o'r vrwyder. A Gruffud a'e niuer a'e hemlynvs enteu trwy vaestired a mynyded hyt ar gyfinyd e wlat e hun.

Ac o'r achaus hvnnv y drycheuit Gruffud o'r dyd hvnnv allan, ac y gelwit o'e obryn en vrenhin Gwyned. Ac e llawenhaus enteu megys cavr y redec y ford, gan rydhau Gvyned o'r argluydi a dothoed idi o le arall, ac a oedent en e gvledychu en enwir; megys yd amdiffynnvs Iudas Machabeus gulat er Israel y gan y brenhined paganyeit a'r kenedloed kyttervyn, a ruthrei en eu plith en venych. A guede gvneithur y velly pob peth, y dechreuws Gruffud gvastatau y deyrnas a llunyethu y gverin, ac eu llywyav yg gvyalen haearnaul yn ogonyanhus en er Argluyd.

[Ymosod ar gastell Rhuddlan]

A guede llithrav odena ychydic o amser, o annoc gvyrda y wlat y kynnvllws llu maur, ac y kerdus parth a chastell Rudlan y emlad a Robert castellwr, ac a'r marchogyon ereill dywal o Freinc a dothoedent y diwed hvnnv y Loegyr, ac odena a dothoedent y wledychu kyffinyd Gwyned. A guede bydinav ohonav a dyrchauael y arwydyon, yd anreithyus y bailli ac y lloskes ac y duc anreith vaur. [7] Llawer o varchogyon llurugauc a helmauc o'r Freinc a diguydassant y ar eu meirch en emlad, a llawer o bedyt, a breid y diengis ychydic onadunt en e twr. A phan gigleu vrenhin Ywerdon a'e varwneit bot mor hyrwyd damwein Gruffud eu car ac eu mab maeth a henne, e llawenhaassant wynteu en vawr.

[Brwydr Bron yr Erw]

Ac odena tri meib Merwyd a holwyr Lleyn a diunassant en erbyn Gruffud eu hargluyd priodaur, ac a ladassant hyt nos en eu lletyeu en e wlat o'r Gwydyl deudengwyr a deugeint o varchogyon Gruffud a'e deulu. A phan gigleu Trahaearn henne, en orchyuygedic ac en foedic, llawenhau a oruc o dyvu er anvundep hvnnv y rung Gruffud a'e wyr. Ac en e lle y kerdus enteu ar wyr Powys, ac annoc udunt dyuot y gyt ac ef am benn Gwyned

31

en amylder torvoed, y dial arnadunt Kenwric y
gar. Ac urth henne y doeth Gurgeneu m. Seissyll,
brenhin Powys a'e niuer, y gyt a Trahaearn a'e
niuer enteu, o gytduvndep y uynnv goresgyn
brenhinyaeth Gruffud vrenhin. A phan glgleu tri
meib Merwyd a gvyr Lleyn ac Eiuyonyd henne, y
bredychassant wynteu Gruffud vrenhin, eu hargluyd
priodaur, megys guyr anudonyl anfydlavn, a
chanorthuyau eu gelynyon a bot en dywyssogyon
udunt y'r kyuoeth. A deu vroder o Von, Tuder a
Gollwyn, a wnaethant en gyffelip y henne, wedy
kemryt eu kyuarws yg Kellynnauc Vaur y gan
Gruffud.

A phan gigleu Gruffud y brat a'r dvundap a oed
en e erbyn y gan y wyr e hun y gyt a'e elynyon, y
doeth en eu herbyn a guyr Mon ac Arvon ac
ychydic o wyr Denmarc a'r Gvydyl ganthav, a
bruydyr dirvaur a gyuodes. Aerua vaur a vu o
bop parth, a llawer a digvydassant o lu Gruffud
vrenhin, a llawer a dalyassant en e vrwydyr, -
Cerit y datmaeth, a Varudri, tywyssauc y Gwydyl
ac argluyd Cruc Brenan (sef lle oed hvnnv
goruchel venyd Seint Brendan, hermidur anryued,
a naw cantref en e gylch). Ac o oreuguyr Mon y
digvydassant dengwyr a thriugeint. Ac eissyoes,
Gruffud vrenhin en eisted ar y varch en e vedin,
a'e gledyf llathreit en medi a'e vratwyr a'e
elynyon, megys Agamemnon, brenhin Frigia, gynt
en emlad Tro. [8] Ac ena e kyrchus Tuder, guas
o Von, penn bratwr Ruffud, gan frydyav gleif, ac
y trosses kyueillyorn ef y'u gyrchu en e goryf ol
y'u gyfrwy. A phan weles Gvyncu, barwn o Von,
henne, y tynnvs ef o'r urwyder o'e anuod hyt y
long a oed en Abermenei. Ac odena yd aethant
hyt en enys Adron, sef lle oed hvnnv enys y
moelronyeit. Odena hyt en Llwch Garmavn en
Ywerdon y kerdassant. A'r gyvranc honno er

henne hyt hediv a elwir Bronn yr Erv, neu Erw yr Allt er henne hyt hediv.

Na ryvedet y bobyl, hagen, bot gueithyeu gorvot a gueithyeu fo y'r tywyssogyon herwyd damwein, canys brat ysyd er y dechreu. Val henne y gvnaeth pobyl yr Israel, a vredychassant ac a rodassant eu brenhin dyledauc ac eu hargluyd, nyt amgen Iudas Machabeus, y Demetrius brenhin anfydlavn; ac enteu eissyoes, val emladwr Duw, kyffelip y gavr ac y lew, a emdialws e hun en da o'r dwy bleit. Ulkessar, amperauder Ruuein, wedy goresgyn ohonav er holl vyt a'e wastatav o emladeu, y lladaud senedwyr Ruvein ef o vrat a phuyntleu yg Cabidyldy Ruvein. Arthur heuyt, brenhin brenhined enys Brydein a rysswr honneit clotvaur, a wnaeth deudec prif emlad en erbyn y Saesson a'r Fichtyeit, ac en e gentaf onadunt y bu orchyuygedic a foavder ef o achaus brat yg Caer Lwytcoet, sef lle oed hvnnv dinas e llwyn llwyt. En cr emladeu ereill y bu vudugaul enteu, ac y talws e'r Saesson a'r Fichtyeit y ormeswyr, ket bei henwr ef, chuyl teilung en e gurthuynep.

[Ymgyrch arall]

A guedy dyuot Gruffud Ywerdon, y kwynws en dost urth y brenhin a'e dywyssogyon rac y vratwyr a'e ormeswyr. Ac aniodef vu ganthunt wynteu henne, a'e annoc a orugant idav y emchuelut dracheuyn en gyflym a llynges gyweir o reidwyf a reidyeu ac emladwyr. Ac urth henne enteu a emchuelus parth a'e wlat gan rwygav dyvynvoroed, a deng llong ar ugeint llavn o Wydyl a gvyr Denmarc; ac en Abermenei e disgynnassant. Ac ena y caussant Trahaearn en guledychu en e wlat.

A phan gigleu Trahaearn ry dyuot y llynges vrenhinyaul, tristau ac ucheneidyav a oruc, ac ergryn ac ouyn a'e dygyrchus. A mudav guyr

Lleyn ac Arduduy ac eu da a oruc atav hyt yg cantref Meiryonnyd, a gavas onadunt. [9] A Gruffud enteu a'e lu a dugant y rann arall o Leyn ac Arvon hyt ym Mon, val y gellynt bot eno en diogel a dan y amdiffyn ef.

Odena y llidyus y Daynysseit ef guyr y dy a'e dylwyth e hun, cany cheynt eu gordyfneit mal yr adawadoed udunt. Ac yd anreithyassant can mwyaf Mon y dreis y arnav, ac emchuelut y eu gvlat ac eu llongeu en llavn o deneon a goludoed, a'e dwyn enteu ganthunt, ac nyt o'e vod. Ac ny bu lei ena y Gruffud brat y Daenysseit noc vn y Gemry.

[Y Normaniaid yn anrheithio Gwynedd]
Odena y tyvaud llawer o drwc a govut yg Gwyned. Ac emplith henne, wede ychydic o amser, y kynullvs Hu yarll Caer a llawer o dywyssogyon ereill, nyt amgen Robert o Rudlan, a Gvarin o Amwythic, a Guallter yarll Henford, y llu mvyaf en e byt o varchogyon a phedyt. Ac a dugant ganthunt Gurgeneu m. Seissyll a gvyr Powys, ac a gerdassant y mynyded ene doethant hyt en Lleyn. Ac en e cantref hvnnv y lluestassant wythnos, gan y distryv beunyd a'e hanreithyav a llad aerva vaur o galaned y hadaussant. Ac odena y bu diffeith e wlat wyth mlyned. Ac odena pobel y wlat honno a wascarassant en dielw ar hyt y byt yn reidussyon. A llawer onadunt a aethant alltuded y wladoed ereill trwy hir vlwydyned, ac o vreid y doeth nep onadunt y eu gvlat. A honno vu y bla gentaf a dyvodyat agarw y Nordmannyeit yn gentaf y daear Wyned, wedy eu dyvodyat y Loegyr.

[Cynghrair â Rhys ap Tewdwr]
Ac en henne, wedy bot Gruffud bluydyned en

Ywerdon megys yn trwydet y gyt a Diermit
vrenhin ac y gyt a'r guyrda ereill, en e diwed ef a
gynnvllus llynges vrenhinyaul o Borthlarc a
rodassei y brenhin idav, en llavn o Daenysseit a
Gvydyl a Brytanyeit. A guedy lledu hwyllyeu ar e
mor, a'r gvynt en hyrwyd oc eu hol, a'r mor en
dangneuedus, ef a doeth y Borth Cleis ker llaw
archescopty Mynyv.

Ac ena y kerdus Rys m. Teudur, brenhin
Deheubarth Kemry, a'r escop a'e athraon a holl
clas er argluyd Dewi ac vn eglvys Vynyv, hyt e
borth. A Rhys gentaf a emadrodes val hynn a'r
argluyd Gruffud: 'Hanbych well Gruffud, brenhin
brenhined Kemry! Atat ti yd wyf vi en fo. Rac
dy vronn y digvydaf ar dal vy glinyeu y erchi dy
ganorthvy a'th nerth.'   'Pwy wyt titheu,' hep y
Gruffud, [10] 'ac y ba beth ry doethost ema?'
'Rys wyf vi,' hep enteu, 'm. Teudur, argluyd y
kyuoeth hvnn ychydic kynn no hynn.   Ac er aur
hon en urthladedic ac en foedic ac en divlanedic
haeach, yd wyf en emdirgelu en e nodua honn.'
'Pwy a'th foes di?' hep y Gruffud. 'Argluyd,' hep
enteu, 'tri brenhin o'r gwladoed pennaf o Gemry
ac eu lluoed a disgynnassant y'm kyuoeth y diwed
hvnn, a pheunyd e maent en y hanreithyav,' 'Pwy,'
hep e Gruffud, 'y brenhined a gerdant trwy dy
wyr di a'th gyuoeth mor vydinauc a henne?'
'Caradauc m. Gruffud,' heb enteu, 'o Went Uch
Coet ac Is Coet a'e Wenhvyssyon, a gvyr Morgannvc, a llawer o albryswyr Nordmannyeit ganthav;
Meilir m. Riwallaun a'e Bowyswyr ganthav,
Trahaearn vrenhin a gwyr Arwystli.'

A phan gigleu Gruffud enw y ormeswyr, froeni
o gyndared a oruc, a govyn idav pa beth a rodei
er emlad drostav en erbyn y gvyr henne. 'Dyoer,'
heb y Rys, 'hanner vyg kyuoeth a rodaf yt, ac y
gyt a henne guryogaeth a wnaf yt.'   A chyvun a

35

henne vu Gruffud. A guedy y kyfruch hvnnv, wynt a gerdassant y gyt y egluys Dewi yn eu guedi. Ac eno yd emwnaethant en gyueillyon fydlavn trwy aruoll y greiryeu.

[Brwydr Mynydd Carn]

A guedy emdivnav onadunt en e lle honno a chemryt bendith er escop, Gruffud a gerdus en er vn dyd hvnnv racdav, ef a'e Daenysseit a'e Wydyl a llawer o Wyndit riuedi wyth ugeinwyr, a Chendelu m. Conus o Von oc eu blaen. Rys enteu ac ychydic Deheuwyr a gerdus gyt ac wy, en llawen ganthav y vryt o'e ganhorthvy.

A guedy kerdet dirvaur emdeith diwyrnaut, yg kylch gosper wynt a doethant y venyd, en e lle yd oed lluesteu y dywededigyon vrenhined uchof. Ac ena y dywaut Rys urth Ruffud vrenhin, 'Argluyd,' hep ef, 'annodun y vrvyder hyt avory, canys gosper yu er aur honn, a'r dyd ysyd en trengi.' 'Annot di,' hep y Gruffud dan igyon, 'os mynny. Mivi a'm bydin a ruthraf udunt hwy.' Ac y velly y bu. A dechrynv a orugant y brenhined eissyoes, val y guelsant y torvoed budugaul amravael a bedinoed Gruffud vrenhin a'e arwydyon yn eu herbyn, a gvyr Denmarc ac eu bwyeill deuvinyauc, a'r Guydyl gaflachauc ac eu peleu haearnaul kyllellauc, a'r Gwyndyt gleiuyauc tareanauc.

[11] Gruffud gentaf emladwr a gyrchus y vrwyder en gyffelip y gaur ac y lew, hep orfowys o danu y urthuynepwyr o gledyf lluchyadennaul. Gyrru grymm en e wyr a oruc ac eu gelynyon en wraul, a hyt na rodynt udunt eu kefneu o nep ryw uod. Ac ena y bu vrwyder dirvaur y chof y'r etiued wedy eu ryeni. Geuri er emladwyr a dyrchauwyt y'r awyr: seinnyav a oruc y daear gan duryf y meirch a'r pedyt: y sein emladgar a glywyt ympell: kynnvryf er arveu a seinnyei en

venych: gvyr Gruffud en dwyssav en wychyr, ac
eu gelynyon en darystung udunt: chwys y llavur
a'r gvaet en gvneithur frydeu redegauc. Ac en
henne, Trahaearn a drychut en e gymperved, eny
ytoed y'r llaur en varw, en pori a'e danhed y
llyssyeu ir ac en palualu ar warthaf er arveu; a
Gucharki Wydel a wnaeth bacwn ohonav ual o
hwch. Ac en er vn lle hvnnv e digvydassant en e
gylch o'e deulu e hun pymp marchauc ar ugeint.
Rei ereill onadunt a las en e vedin gentaf. Llawer
o uilyoed onadunt a las, a'r lleill a rodassant eu
kefneu y wyr Gruffud ac a emchuelassant ar fo.
Gruffud enteu, o'e gnotaedic deuaut, en vudugaul
a'e hemlynvs wynteu, ef a'e niuer, trvy y llwyneu
a'r glynnyeu a'r guerni a'r mynyded en hyt e nos
honno urth y lleuat, ac en hyt e dyd drannoeth. A
breid vu o diengis nep onadunt o'r vrwyder y eu
gvlat e hunein.

A guedy darvot y vrwyder, ofynhav brat o
barthret Gruffud a oruc Rys. Ymdynnv a dan gel
kyfliw gur a llwyn a oruc o gedymdeithas Gruffud
a'e wyr, ac nyt emdangosses y nep onadunt o
henne allan. Ac am henne y sorres Gruffud, ac
am henne yd erchis Gruffud y'u wyr anreithyav
kyuoeth Rys. Ac y velly e darvu.

E menyd, hagen, y bu e vrwyder endav a eilw
kiudaut e wlat Menyd Carn. Sef yu henne menyd
e garned; canys eno e mae diruaur garned o vein,
a dan er honn y cladwt rysswr yg kynnoessoed
gynt.

A guede gvneithur dirvaur bla eno a llawer o
anreithyeu, e kerdus Gruffud parth ac Arwystli ac
y distrywyus ac y lladaud y guerin; ac y lloskes y
thei, a'e gvraged a'e morynnyon a duc yg
keithiwet. Ac y velly e talws y chvyl y Drahaearn.
Odena y kerdus y Bowys, en e lle e dangosses ar
hynt [12] y greulonder y'u urthuynepwyr o devaut
budugaul; ac nyt arbedus keuei yr egluysseu. A

37

guede llad y uelly y elynyon a distriv eu daear en gubel, yd emchuelus y'u briodolder a thref y dat e hun, y'u medu ac y'u thagneuedu. Ac y bu orfowys a heduch yg Gvyned ychydic o dieuoed.

[Carcharu Gruffud]

Ac val yd oed y uelly en arver o uwynnyant y vrenhinyaeth, y kyffroet Meiryaun Goch o saeth diauwl, y varwn e hun, ac y kuhudus ef urth Hu yarll Caer, ac y bredychus en e mod hvnn. Peri a oruc y deu yarll o Freinc, nyt amgen, er Hu a dywetpvyt uchof a Hu yarll Amvythic, mab Royzer o Gastell Baldwin, dyvot y gyt ac amylder marchogyon a phedyt ganthunt, hyt y Ruc en Edeirnyavn. Y bradwr, hagen, a'e bredychvs ef o'r geiryeu hynn, 'Argluyd,' heb ef, 'mae deu yarll o'r ardal y'th annerch ac y'th wediav, am dy dyuot en diogel gyt a'th wyr dieither y gyfruch ac wynt hyt yg Gruc yn Edeirnyavn.' A Gruffud, gan gredu er emadrodyon henne, a doeth hyt en lle y deilly-adaeth. A phan weles yr yeirll ef, e daleassant ac ef a'e niuer, ac y dodassant ef yg geol Gaer e carchar guaethaf, a geuynneu arnav, deudeng blyned. Y wir dieither enteu, wedy eu dale, a dorret y uaut deheu y lav pob vn onadunt; ac y val henne y gadasant wy emdeith. A phan glywyt henne, y guascarassant y lleill; canys emadraud duywaul a dyweit: 'Mi a drawaf y bugeil, a deueit y genveint a wascarant.'

[Ei berson]

Kedemdeitheon gvahanredaul Gruffud a dywedynt y uot ef en wr kymedraul y veint, a gvallt melyn arnav, ac emennyd guressauc ac wynep crwnn, da y liw, a llygeit maur guedus, ac aeleu tec, a baryf wedus, a mvnugyl crwnn, a chnaut gvynn, ac aelodeu grymus, a byssed hiryon, ac esgeiryeu

38

vnyaun, a thraet tec. Kywreint oed a huaudel en
amravaellyon yeithyoed. Bonhedic oed enteu, a
thrugarauc urth y givdaut, a chreulavn urth y
elynyon, a gwychraf em bruyder.

[Hu iarll yng Ngwynedd]

Ac en e lle wedy e dale ef, e doeth Hu yarll
y'u gyuoeth enteu en amylder torvoed, ac y
gvnaeth kestyll a lleoed cadarn o deuaut y Freinc,
a bot en argluyd ar e tir. Castell a oruc e Mon,
ac arall en Arvon en hen gaer Custennin amperauder, vab Constans Vaur. Arall a wnaeth ym
Bangor ac arall ym Meiryonnyd. Ac a ossodes
endunt mar[13]chogyon a phedyt seithydyon,
a chemeint a wnaethant o drwc ac na wnaethpuyt
y gyfryu er dechreu y byt. A llef y bobyl a
esgynnvs ar er Argluyd, ac enteu a'e guerendewis
wy.

[Dianc o'r carchar: cyrraedd Iwerddon]

Ac en henne y kerdus heibyau vn vlyned ar
bemthec, ac e rydhaut Gruffud o'e garchar. Canys
guryanc o Edeirnyavn (Kenwric Hir oed y enw) a
doeth y Gaer, ac ychydic o gedemdeitheon y gyt
ac ef, y brynv eu hangenreidyeu. A phan weles
enteu en evynnauc ym plas e dinas, y kemyrth ar
y geuyn ef ac y duc hep wybot. Ac y kerdus y
emdeith ef a'e gedemdeitheon pyrnavn, pan ytoed
y burgeissyeit en bwyta, ac y porthes en e dy e
hun ef rynnavd o dydyeu a dan gel. A guede
tervyn dieuoed a chryfhau Gruffud, y duc ef y
nos hyt e Mon, ac ena e diwalus Sandef vab Ayre
ef yg kud.

Ac odena, wede ychydic o dydyeu, yd esgynnvs y
long y vynnv mynet Ywerdon. Ac eissyoes y
gurthwynt a'e duc hyt ym Porth Hodni en Deheubarth. Odena y kerdus e'r tir a nav kedemdeith

etholedic ganthau, a'r nauvet a las ar hynt.
Kivdaut y wlat honno a emladus ac ef teir gueith
e dyd hvnnv, a'r teir gueith henne y gorvu ef
arnadunt hwy, ef a'e wyth gedemdeith; a llad
ohonav enteu e hvn vn o'r gueissyon bonhedicaf a
hanoed o'r kyuoeth hunnv. Ac y velly y dienghis
y ganthunt. Odena, ar y kerdet hvnnv, y doeth
hyt en Arduduy, en bedrus ganthav pa le y kyrchei
rac brat y Freinc. A phan y gueles meibeon
Gollwyn ef, Eginir, Gellan, Merwyd, Edneuet, y
truanassant urthau, ac y diwallassant ef a dan gel
y mevn gogoueu diffeith. A guedy diwed missoed
e dvvnassant idav wyth ugeinwyr, ac y krwydr-
assant o le i le yg Gwyned, can wneithur colledeu
yn oes yr yarll Hu, megys Dauid vrenhin, mab
Ysai, o Vethlem yg gulat Iudea en oes Saul vrenhin.
A guedy guelet o'r Freinc a oed ena en e kestyll
evo en afryoli y velly, eu hemlyn a wnaethant ac
wynt a chivdaut e wlat yg coet ac y maes, megys
gellgvn neu callgun en hely ac en dilit carv blin.
A phan adnabu enteu na allei emdianc y velly, yd
aeth en yscraff e canonwyr en Aberdaron, ac en
honno a dan rwyf yd aeth hyt en Ywerdon.
Odeno eilchuyl ym pen y mis y doeth dracheuyn
en [14] er vn yscraff, ac y cavas aber er vn avon
o'r lle y kychvynnassei. Ac odeno y kerdus
eilweith dracheuen hyt en Ywerdon.

[Adennill Gwynedd]

Ac odeno, wedy kemryt kyngor, y kerdus o hwyl
a rwyf hyt en enyssed Denmarc ar Gothrei vrenhin
y gyveillt, y adolwyn idav llongeu ac eu doodreuyn
ac eu reidyeu; canys ena gentaf ry dothoed atav
gan emdiryet y geissyav porth. Ac enteu a gan-
orthvyws idav ef, gan gytdiodef a chytdoluryav
a'e uenych berygleu ef.
Ac odena y kerdus Gruffud a thriugein llong

ganthav, ac y doeth hyt e Mon y arvaethu ef a gvyr er enyssed emlad a chastell y Freinc. A gvyr e wlat a vuant ormod llesteir udunt. Ac ena y bu urwyder lidyawc, creulavn, galet o'r bore hyt byrnhavn, a llawer a digvydassant o bop parth, a'r gvyr deurhaf en gentaf. Ac emplith henne neidyav a oruc Gruffud o'r blaen en e vydin gentaf y drychu y Freinc llurugauc a helmauc o'e uwyall deuvinyauc, vegys Dauyd vrenhin emplith y Philistewyssyon. A'r nos a wahanvs y vrvyder.

A guedy daruot e vrwyder, y llongeu a gerdassant y'r enyssed. Evo hagen, ac vn llong ganthav, a drigyus en Ron enys, nyt amgen enys dinewyt e mor, ac a yspeillyus llong en dyuot o Gaer, a llad y guerin. A thrannoeth ef a hwyllyus parth a Lleyn, ac a doeth y borth Nevyn. A phan gigleu wyr y cantreuoed henne, dyuot ar vrys a orugant atav gvyr Lleyn ac Eiuyonyd ac Arduduy ac Arvon a Ros a Dyfrynt Cluyt, a'e arvoll, mal y deleynt eu hargluyd dyledauc. A guedy cadarnhau Gruffud o lu maur en e gylch trvy nerth Duw, e damgylchynvs e castell a dywetpuyt uchot, a oed y Mon, ac a emladus ac ef rynnavd o dydyeu, a'r Freinc oc eu keyryd ac eu kedernyt ac eu tyroed en burv ergydyeu a saytheu ac a chuareleu ac a thafleu ac a magneleu en gawadeu. Ac eissyoes eu gorchyuygu a wnaethpuyt udunt o beunydyawl emlad e Kemry. Eu hystiwart llys a las, er hvnn a oed en medu y castell, a phetwar guyr a chue ugeint o varchogyon y gyt ac ef.

A guedy lloski e castell a goruot ar y gelynyon, llawenhau a oruc Gruffud, a cherdet am benn y kestyll ereill a oedent en lleoed ereill en e deyrnas, ac emlad ac wynt, ac eu lloski, ac eu torri, [15] a llad eu guerin endunt em pob lle. Rydhav Gvyned a oruc o'e chestyll a chemryt y

gyuoeth idav e hun, a thalu eu chuyl en deilung
y'u urthuynebwyr. A heduch vu Wyned ena dwy
vlyned.

A choffa hynn heuyt: pan ytoed Gruffud en
emlad a chastell Aberllienyauc y Mon, ar y chue
ugeinvet o wyr a phetwar ar dec o veibeon yeueinc,
y loski ohonav a'e anreithyav a llad llawer o'r
castellwyr; a guede y anreithyav en llwyr,
emchuelut hyt e tu arall y Von yd oed teir llong
idav. A'r castellwyr a gvyr Mon a'e hemlynassant
enteu en hyt e dyd, gan vrvydrav en y ol en
wychyr. Ac val kynt y kerdassant wynteu
dracheuyn a'r anreith, ac a Freinc a Saesson en
rwym ganthunt ac en garcharoryon, a llawer oc
eu hemlynwyr a ladassant o'r hir vrwyder. Ac
ena y diguydus Gellan telynyaur penkerd o
barthret Gruffud en e llynges.

Pa den, yr y gyuaruydet a'e drybelitet, a allei
mynegi en llwyr kyfrangeu Gruffud a'e ryueloed y
rung Kemry ac Ywerdon ac enyssed Denmarc ac
amravaellyon genedloed ereill. Mivi a gyuadeuaf
nas dichonaf vi, ac nas dichonvn, pei bedvn kyn
huotlet a Thullius vard ym prol ac a Maro vard
en traethaut mydyr.

[Ei wraig a'e blant]

Ac val yd oed Gruffud y velly weithieu en rwyd,
weithyeu en afruyd racdav, ef a gemyrth gureic,
Angharat y henv, merch y Ewein vab Edwin, er
honn a dywedynt doethyon y kyuoeth y bot en
vonhedic, hyduf, walltwenn, lygatvras, oskethloyu,
a chorff gualcheid, ac aelodeu grymus, ac
esgeiryeu hyduf, a'r traet goreu, a byssed hiryon,
ac ewined teneu; hynavs, a huaudel, a da o uwyt
a llynn, a doeth a chall, a chynghorwreic da,
trugarauc urth y chyuoeth, a chardodus urth
achanogyon, a chyfreithus ym pob peth.

42

Ac o honno y bu idav meibeon a merchet. Enw y meibeon vu Catwallavn, ac Ewein, a Chatwalader; a'e verchet oed Guenlliant a Maryret, a Rainillt, a Sussanna, ac Annest. Ef a vu veibeon a merchet idav heuyt o gatyatwraged.

[Ymgyrch Gwilym Gleddyf Hir]
A phan gigleu Guillim Gledyf Hir, brenhin Lloeger, miluryaeth Gruffud a'e dywalder a'e greulonder en erbyn e Freinc, aniodef vu ganthav. A chyffroi a oruc y holl deyrnas en e erbyn, a dyuot hyt yg Gwyned en amylder torvoed marchogyon [16] a phedyt, gan arvaethu dileu a distryw paub o'r givdaut en llwyr hyt na bei en vyw kemeint a chi. Ef heuyt a arvaethassei torri yr holl goedyd a'r llwyneu, hyt na bei wascaut nac amdiffyn e'r Gwyndyt o henne allan. Ac urth henne e lluestws ac y pebyllyus en gentaf em Mur Castell, a rei o'r Kemry en gyuarwydyeit idav. A phan gigleu Gruffud henne, y kynullvs enteu llu y holl vrenhinyaeth, ac y kerdus en e erbyn ef, urth wneithur ragotvaeu idav en lleoed keuing pan disgynnei o'r menyd. Ac ouynhau henne a oruc enteu, a chyuarchuelut y lu trwy berued y wlat eny doeth y Gaer, hep wneithur nep kyfryu gollet en er hynt honno y givdaut y wlat. Ac ny chavas ganthav nep kyfryu frwyth nac enill, namen vn vuch; a cholli rann vaur o varchogyon ac acueryeit a gueissyon a meirch, a llawer o daoed ereill. Ac y velly e dielws ryuyc y Freinc hyt ar dim.

Ac en henne uyth Gruffud a'e lu ganthunt, weithyeu o'r blaen, weithyeu en ol, weithyeu ar deheu, weithyeu ar assw udunt, rac gvneithur onadunt nep ryw gollet en e kyuoeth. A phei as ry atei Gruffud y'u wyr emgymyscu ac wynt ar y llwyneu, diwethaf dyd uydei hvnnv y vrenhin

43

Lloegyr a'e Freinc. Enteu, hagen, a arbedus idav
ef, megys Dauyd vrenhin gynt y Saul.

[Ymgyrch yr ieirll]
A guedy daruot henne, Hu yarll Caer, er hvnn a
dywetpuyt uchot, gureid er holl drwc megys
Antiochus gynt, a gynullus llynges a llu diruaur
anryued y'r wlat, gan dristit a chwynvan a dolur
a choffau y gastellwyr, a diwreidyau y gestyll a
lladua e varchogyon. Ac a gytduvnvs ac ef Hu
arall, yarll Amvythic, a'e lu enteu, val e delynt
y gyt en gyvun e dial e colledeu ry wnathoed
Gruffud udunt. Ac urth henne e kerdassant ac eu
llu en eu llynges ar vor hyt yg kyuoeth Gruffud,
ac Ewein vab Edwin ac Uchdryt y vravt oc eu
blaen ac eu gallu. A phan vu honneit henne, guyr
Gwyned a Phowys a gytduvnassant y urthwynebu
udunt hep darystung. Ac urth henne y mudassant
argluydi Powys, nyt amgen, Cadugavn a Maredud
y vravt, ac eu hanhedeu ganthunt hyt ar Gruffud.
Ac ena wedy [373] kymryt kytgyngor ydd
aethant hyt y Mon, ag wynt a Gruffudd, ag yno
ydd ymddifferassant megis y mewn kaer a vei
damgylchynedig o weilgi. Kanys y Ruffudd ry
ddothoedd un llong ar bymtheg o gyfareu hirion
yn borth iddaw o Ywerddon, a'r rei hynny y
vrwydraw ar for yn erbyn llynges yr yeirll. A
phan ddoeth hynny ar yr yeirll, ydd anfonassant
wynteu kennadeu hyt ar y llongeu ry ddothoedd
y gannorthwyaw Gruffudd, y erchi uddunt pallu
iddaw pan vei kyfyngaf arnaw, a dyfot attaddunt
wynteu yr a fynnynt o dda. Ag y felly y darfu.
Wedy kredu onaddunt [374] y dwyll y Ffreink, y
tywalldassant oll yr ynys, gan torri eu harfoll
wrth Ruffudd.
A phan wybu Ruffudd hynny, doluryaw a chymrawu
yn fawr a orug, kany wyddyat pa gynghor a wnei

44

yn erbyn y wrthwynebwyr o Ffreink a'r brat
longheu. Ag yna, wedy mynet yg kyngor ef a
Chadwgawn fab Bleddynt y daw, y kerddassant y
mewn ysgraff yny ddoethant hyt yn Ywerddon, ag
adaw eu kiwdawt ag a oedd eiddunt yn ewyllys
Duw a'e amddiffyn, yr hwn a notaa kannorthwyaw
y bob dyn pan vo kyfyngaf arnunt o anebryfegedig
rubuchet. A phan wybu eu pobyl wynteu hynny,
ydd ymchwelassant ar ffo, gan ymddirgelu ag
ymguddiaw y gogofeu daearawl, a gwerni, a
choedydd, a llwyneu, a rhedynossydd, ag elltydd,
a diffwysseu, a chorsydd, a drysswch, a cherrig,
ag ym pob rhyw leoedd ereill o'r y gellynt
ymguddyaw rhag ofyn yr Iddewon, nit amgen, y
Ffreink a chenedloedd ereill ry ddothoeddynt yng
kyrch uddunt. Kanys megys y dyweit dwywawl
ymadrawdd: 'digwyddaw a orug y bobyl hep
tywyssawg.' Ag ny bu ohir, yr yeirll ag eu lluoedd
ag [375] eu hemlynassant wynteu yn orawenus y
dydd hwnnw hyt ucher ar hyt ag ar llet yr ynys,
gan y hanreithyaw a lladd y gwerin a thorri
aelodeu ereill. A'r nos a wastataws yr ymlit.

[Ymddangosiad Magnus frenin]
    A thrannoeth, nachaf trwy weledigaeth Duw
llynges vrenhinawl yn agos yn ddirybudd yn
ymddangos. A phan welet honno, anhyfrydu a
orug y Ffreink a'r Daenysseit bratwyr a dwylles-
synt Ruffud. Ag fal ydd oedd vradawg y Ffreink
eissyoes yn wastat, ydd anfonassant wynteu a dan
gel yn y lle rei o'r Kymry kyfun ag wynt hyt ar
wyr yr ynys, y erchi uddunt ar vrys ddyfod y
dangnefedd, a rhoddi diogelrwydd uddunt; kanys
ofyn vu ganthunt gorfot arnaddunt o'r Kymry
ffoedigion o'r neill parth, a'r llynges vrenhinawl
o'r parth arall. Ag y felly y darfu. Ag y felly
y twyllws y Ffreink bratwyr y Kymry o bob parth

gwarchaedigyon yn yr ynys, wedy y bla ry
wnathoeddynt a allei dyfot ar gof y'r etifedd
wedy y ryeni.

[Marw Hu iarll Amwythig]
E llynges hagen, ry welsynt hwy yn ddeissyfyt,
brenhin Llychlyn bieuoedd, [376] a gyvarwyddassei
Duw o'e trugaredd y Fon, y ryddhau y bobyl
warchaedig gan yr angkyfyeith; kanys galw ry
wnathoeddynt ar eu Harglwydd yn eu dioddeifeint
ag eu gofit, a Duw ag eu gwerendewis. A gwedy
datkanu y'r brenhin trwy yeithydd pa ynys oedd, a
phwy oedd argluydd, pa anrheithyaw, a pha
emlynnu, pwy yr emlynwyr, kytdoluryaw a orug,.
a llidiaw, a dynessau y'r tir a their llong. A'r
Ffreink hagen, yn ofnawg fel gwragedd, pan
welsant hynny, a ymladdassant yn llurygawg, ag
eistedd ar eu meirch og eu defawt, a cherddet y
tu a'r brenhin a nifer y teir llong. A'r brenhin
a'e nifer yn rhyfygus a ymladdws yn eu herbyn
wynteu, a digwyddaw a orug y Ffreink y ar eu
meirch fal ffrwyth y ffigys y ar eu gwydd, rhei
yn feirw, rhei yn vrathedig o ergy[377]dyeu y
Llychlynwyr. A'r brenhin y hun, yn ddigyffro o'r
kwrr blaen y'r llong, a vrathws a saeth Hu yarll
Amwythig yn y lygat, ag ynteu a ddigwyddws o'e
ochrum y'r ddaear yn vriwedig ddieneit y ar y
farch arfawg, dan ymffustyaw ar y arfeu. Ag o'r
damwein hwnnw ydd ymchwelws y Ffreink ar ffo,
a rhoddi eu kefneu y ergyL377dyeu y Llychlynwyr.
A'r brenhin a'e lynghes a hwylyassant oddyno
ymdeith, kanys ef ry ddoethoedd a gallu mawr
ganthaw y edrech ynys Brydein ag Ywerddon, y
rhei ysydd oddi eithyr y byt, megys y dyfot
Fferyll bot y Brytanyeit yn ddieithredig yn gubyl
o'r holl vyt.

[Y Normaniaid a'r bradwyr]

Ag wrth hynny, Hu yarll a'r Ffreink ereill, yn llawen o ymchwelyat Magnws vrenhin, a ddugant ganthunt y Gwyndyt a'r eiddunt oll yn llwyr hyt yg kantref Ros, rhag ofyn dyfodyat Gruffudd awr pob awr. Ag yna y rhifwyt ysgrybyl pob perchennawg a'e anrheith, ag oddyna eu hanheru, ag a'r hanner y kerddws ef y Gaer.

Eno hagen, ydd oeddynt y bratwyr anudonol o'r Daenysseit a vredychessynt Ruffudd yn aros yr eddiweideon a addawsei Hu uddunt, a cheith o wyr a gwragedd, o weisseon a morynnyon. Ag ynteu a'e talws uddunt hwy megis ffyddlawn y anffyddlawn, yn y kadarnhaei dwywawl lunyeth; kanys neu ry ddaroedd iddaw ar ehang kynullaw holl wrachiot mantach, krwm, kloff, unllygeityawg, gormessawl, diallu, ag eu kynnig uddunt ym pwyth eu bradwryaeth. A phan welsant wynteu hynny, gillwng [378] eu llynghes a wnaethant, a chyrchu y dyfynfor parth ag Ywerddon. Y gwr a oedd yn gwledychu yn yr amser hwnnw a beris anafu rhei onaddunt, a thorri eu haelodeu, a dihol ereill yn ddybryt o'e holl deyrnas.

[Tangnefeddu â Hu iarll Caer]

Ag yn yr amser hwnnw, nachaf Ruffudd o'e notaedig ddefawt yn dyfot o Ywerddon, ac y kafas y holl wlat yn diffeith, a'e chiwdawt wedy ry fynet y le arall. Oddyna ydd anfones kennadeu hyt ar yr yarll Hu, ag y tangnefeddws ag ef; ag yn y kantref hwnnw y rhoddet teir tref iddaw. Ag yno y dug eu vuchedd vulwyddynedd yn dlawt ovudus, gan obeithaw wrth weledigaeth Duw rhagllaw.

[Ymgadarnhau yng Ngwynedd]

Ac oddyna, wedy kerddet blwyddynedd heibiaw,

y kerddws y lys Henri, vrenhin Lloegyr, yr [379] hwnn a vu vrenhin yn nessaf y'w vrawt. A chann hwnnw y kafas ef rubuchet a charyat a chyfatnabot, [o] eiryawl a chyfarwyddyt Erfyn, eskob Bangor. Ag y rhoddes iddaw gan dangnefedd a charyat kantref Lleyn, ag Eifyonydd, ag Ardudwy, ag Arllechwedd, ag wynt ag eu gwerin ag eu hanrheithieid. Ag yn y lle, pan ymchwelws Gruffudd o'r llys, y dug eu kyfannedd y'r gwladoedd hynny, gan y ddiolwch y Dduw, yr hwnn a ddiyt y kywoethogyon syberw og eu kadeir ag a ddyrcheiff y rhei ufydd yn eu lle, yr hwn a wna yr achanawg yn arberthawg, yr hwn a ystwng dyn ag a'e dyrcheif.

Oddyna eissyoes pob dryll y rhwyddhaws pob peth rhag Gruffudd, kanys y obeith oedd yn yr Arglwydd; a pheunydd y llithrynt attaw ereill o Ros ag eu hanrheithyeu ganthunt hep gannyat yarll Kaer, ag amlau y bobyl. Ag yn y vulwyddyn rhag wyneb y kerddws y Von a'e gwerin ganthaw, ag y gwledychws; ag oddyna y'r kymhydoedd ereill. Ag fal hynny y kafas trachefyn o'e grym pob peth yg Wynedd, megis y gwnaeth Makabews fab Matathias gynt yn yr Israel. A dwyn a wnaeth y holl giwdawt o amrafael alltudedd, y rhei a ae[380]-thoeddynt y alltudedd o'r ymlitfa a ddywetpwyt uchot, ag amlau daoedd yg Gwynedd gan lewenydd, megis am wlat yr Israel ag eu hymchwelyat o geithiwet Babilon.

[Ymgyrchoedd Henri frenin]
A molest a gymyrth yr yarll ynddaw o achub y gywoeth a'e oreskyn y felly, hep y gannyat. A phan gigleu vrenhin Lloegyr hynny, rhyfeddu a orug, ag agori y dryssor, a rhoddi treul didlawd y farchogyon a phedit, a dwyn ganthaw vrenhin Yskotlont a'r Yskotyeit a gwyr y Deheu. Ag y

felly y doeth y gywoeth Gruffudd, a phebyllyaw y
Mur Kastell. A Gruffudd ynteu, o genefindra a
brwydyr, a luestws yn y erbyn ynteu ym breichyeu
Eryri eiriawg. Ag oddyno ymanfon a'r brenhin,
ag o'r bren[381]hin ag ynteu trwy yspeit dieuoedd,
a thangnefeddu. Ag oddyna ydd ymchwelws
Henri vrenhin y Loegyr, a Gruffudd y'w gywoeth.

Ag eilweith, wedy rhynnawt o amser, y doeth
Henri vrenhin drachevyn a lluoedd mawr ganthaw,
a phebyllyaw a orug yn yr un lle a ddywetpwyt
uchot yn y mynydd, y arfaethu diwreiddiaw
kywoeth Gruffudd a'e ddistryw, a lladd a difa y
giwdawt yg geneu y kleddyf. A phann glywyt
hynny, wedi kynullaw llu, y doeth Gruffudd yn y
erbyn o'e notaedig ddefawt, a gossot y anheddeu
a'e vileinllu a'r gwragedd a'r meibeon yn drysswch
mynyddedd Yryri, yn y lle ny ddioddefassant un
perygyl. Ag wrth hynny ydd ofynhaws y brenhin
y ddigwyddaw yn llaw Ruffudd o'e pydyaw, pann
ddisgynnei o'r mynydd, [ag] y kerddws drachefyn
gan wneuthur tangnefedd ag ef.

O wi à Duw, y gnifer gweith ydd arfaethassant
yeirll Kaer gwrthwynebu y Ruffudd, ag nys
gallassant! A'r gnifer gweith gwyr Powys, ag nys
gallassant! A'r gnifer gweith gwyr Trahaearn
twyllwr, ag nys gallassant eissyoes y ddwyn ar
gwbylder!

[Heddwch a ffyniant]

A gwedy hynny y gwledychws Gruffudd llawer o
vulwyddynedd yn hyrw[382]ydd gywaethawg gan
arafwch a heddwch, ag yn arfer o gymydogaeth y
brenhinedd nessaf iddaw yn gyfun, nyt amgen
Henri vrenhin Lloegyr, Mwrchath vrenhin Ywerddon,
a brenhin ynyssedd Denmark; a honneit amlwg vu
ag yn y teyrnassoedd pell y wrthaw ag yn y rhei
agos iddaw. Ag oddyna ydd amylhaws pob kyfryw

49

dda yg Gwynedd, ag y dechreuassant y kiwdawtwyr adeilat eglwysseu ym pob kyfeir ynddi, a heu koedydd ag eu plannu, a gwneithur perllanneu a garddeu ag eu damgylchynu o gaeu a ffosydd, a gwneithur adeiladeu murddin, ag ymborth o ffrwytheu y ddaear o ddefawt gwyr Rhufein. A Gruffudd ynteu a wnaeth eglwysseu mawr yn y llyssoedd pennaf idaw e hun, ag adeiladoedd y lyssoedd a gwleddeu yn wastad yn anrhydeddus. Pa beth hefyd, echtywynygu a wnei Wynedd yna o eglwysseu kalcheit, fal y ffurfafen o'r syr.

Llywyaw y bobyl a wnaei y gwialen haearnawl, gan wneithur kiundep a thangnefedd a'r teyrnassoedd nessaf iddaw. A'e feibeon, etwa yn weisseon yefeink, a ossodes ar y kantrefoedd eithaf iddaw, y ragfeddu ag [383] y eu kynnal mal mur agkyffroedig yn erbyn estrawn genedloedd a rhei agkyfyeith, o darffei uddunt meddylyaw kyfodi o newydd yn y erbyn. A'r brenhinedd bychein ereill a gyrchynt y lys ef a'e amddiffyn, y kyrchu y ganorthwy a'e gynghor y gnifer gweith y gofudyei estrawn genetloedd wynt.

[Ymneilltuo a rhannu ei dda]
Ag yn y diwedd, eissyoes, Gruffudd a hynhaws, a cholli trem y lygeit a orug; a rhoddi a orug ynteu y ynni y weithredoedd y trugaredd. Wedy meddylyaw ohonaw enw tragwyddawl o filwryaeth, ef a arfaethws hefyt fynet e hun y le dirgel ysgafalaf, y ddwyn buchedd ddwywawl, a thremygu y holl arglwyddiaeth vydawl yn llwyr.

Ag eissyoes, fal ydd oedd y derfyn y fynet o'r byt hwn yn nessau, galw y feibeon a or[384]lug a llunyethu y farwolaeth, fal y gwnaeth y brenhin Ezechias weith arall. Ag wrth hynny, rhannu a orug y holl dda; a'e gyfyawnder ynteu a bara yn oes oessoedd. Ef a anfones ugein swllt y eglwys

50

Grist yn Dulyn, yn y lle y ganet ac y magwyt, a chymeint a hynny y holl eglwysseu pennaf o Ywerddon. A'r gymeint y eglwys Fynyw, a'r gymeint y fanachlog Gaer, a'r gymeint y fanachlog Amwythig, a mwy no hynny y eglwys Vangor, a deg swllt y Gaergybi, a'r gymeint y Benmon, a'r gymeint y Gelynnawg, a'r gymeint y Enlli, a'r gymeint y Feifod, a'r gymeint y Lan Armawn, a'r gymeint y Ddineirth, ag y lawer o eglwysseu pennaduraf ereill. A roddes ynteu y esgob ag archdiagon, effeirieit ag urddolyon ag athrawon, ag y achanogyon kristyawn, y daoedd hynny a gymynnaf fi y amddiffyn yr Yspryt Glan, yr hwn a wyr pob peth ag a'e hatwen.

[Marwolaeth Gruffudd]
Wrth y ddiwedd ynteu y doethant y gwyr mwyaf a doethaf o'r holl gywoeth, Dafydd eskob Bangor, Symeon archdiagon, gwr addfet o oet a doethinap, prior man[385]achlog Kaer, a llawer o effeirieit ag ysgolheigyon yn iraw y gorff ef ag olew kyssygredig, herwydd gorchymyn Yago ebostol. E feibeon hefyt oedd yno ymplith hynny, ag ynteu yn eu bendigaw wy, ag yn dywedut pa ryw wyr vyddunt rhagllaw, megis Yago padriarch yn bendigaw y feibeon gynt yn yr Eifft. A gorchymyn a orug uddunt bot yn wrawl a gwrthwynebu yn wychyr y eu gelynyon, ar y gyffelyprwydd ynteu yn y ddiwedd ddyddyeu. Eno hefyt ydd oedd Angharat vrenhines, y wreig briawt ynteu, ag iddi y rhoddes ynteu hanner y dda, a dwy randir, a phorthloedd Abermenei. Eno ydd oeddynt y ferchet a rhei o'e neieint, ag y bawb o'r rhei hynny hefyt y rhoddes rhann o'r eiddaw yn ymborth uddunt wedy y ddydd ef.
Kymry a Gwyddyl a gwyr Denmark yntwy a ddrygyrferthassant o ddigwyddedigaeth Gruffudd

51

vrenhin, fegis kwynfan yr Iddeon am Ioswe, fab Nwn. Dwy vlwydd a phetwar ugeint oedd Ruffudd, ag yna y bu farw; ag y Mangor y kladdwyt y mewn yskrin yn y parth assw y'r allawr fawr yn yr eglwys. A gweddiwn [386] ninheu hyt pan orffowysso y eneit ynteu yn yr un peth, nyt amgen yn Duw, y gyt ag eneidieu brenhinedd da ereill yn oes oessoedd. Amen.

THE HISTORY OF GRUFFUDD AP CYNAN.

Here beginneth the old history of Gruffudd,
son of Cynan, son of Iago.

[His birth]
In the days of Edward, king of England, and
Toirrdelbach, king of Ireland, was born Gruffudd,
king of Gwynedd, in Ireland, in the city of Dublin;
and in the commote of Columcille was he reared,
the place called in Irish Sword Choluim-Chille,
which lies three miles from the place where lived
his mother and foster-mother.

[His parents]
His father was Cynan, king of Gwynedd, and his
mother was Ragnailt, daughter of Olaf, king of
the city of Dublin and a fifth part of Ireland.
Gruffudd was, therefore, a most high-born man
by reason of his royal kin and most distinguished
lineage, as the pedigree of his parents testifies
and relates.

[His pedigree on his father's side]
For Gruffudd was son of king Cynan, son of
Iago, son of Idwal, son of Elisedd, son of Meurig,
son of Anarawd, son of Rhodri, son of Etill,
daughter of Cynan from the castle of Dindaethwy,
son of Idwaldyre, son of Cadwaladr Fendigaid, son
of Cadwallon, son of Cadfan, son of Iago, son of
Beli, son of Rhun, son of Maelgwn, son of
Cadwallon Lawhir, son of Einion Yrth, son of king
Cunedda, son of Edern, son of Padern Peisrudd,
son of Tagid, son of Iago, son of Gwyddog, son
of Cain, son of Gorgain, son of Doli, son of
Gwrddoli, son of Dwfn, son of Gorddwfn, son of
Anwerydd, son of Onwedd, son of Difwng, son of

Brychwain, son of Owain, son of Afallach, son of Aflech, son of Beli Mawr.

Rhodri Mawr, son of Merfyn Frych, son of Gwriad, son of Elidir, son of Sanddef, son of Alcwn, son of Tegid, son of Gwair, son of Dwg, son of Llywarch Hen, son of Elidir Lydanwyn, son of Meirchion Gul, son of Gorwst Ledlwm, son of Cenau, son of Coel Godebog, son of Tegfan Gloff, son of Deheweint, son of Urban, son of Gradd, son of Rhifeddel, son of Rhideyrn, son of Eudeyrn, son of Euddigant, son of Eudos, son of Euddolen, son of Afallach, son of Aflach, son of Beli Mawr, son of Manogan, son of Enaid, son of Cerwyd, son of Crydon, son of Dyfnarth, son of Prydain, son of Aedd Mawr, son of Antonius, son of Seiriol, son of Gwrwst, son of Rhiwallon, son of Rhagaw, daughter of Llyr, son of Rhudd, son of Bleiddudd, son of Lliwelydd, son of Brutus Ysgwyd Ir, son of Mymbyr, son of Madog, son of Llocrinus, son of Brut prince from Rome, son of Silvius, son of Ascanius, son of Eneas Ysgwyd Wyn, son of Anchises, son of Capys, son of Assaracus, son of Trois, son of Erictonius, son of Dardanus, son of Jupiter, son of Sadwrn, son of Celius, son of Cretus, son of Ciprius, son of Iauan, son of Japhet, son of old Noah, son of Lamech, son of Methuselah, son of Enoch, son of Jaret, son of Mahalaleel, son of Cainan, son of Enos, son of Seth, son of Adam, son of God.

[His pedigree on his mother's side]
Gruffudd's pedigree on his mother's side: king Gruffudd, son of Ragnailt, daughter of Olaf, king of the city of Dublin and a fifth part of Ireland and the Isle of Man, who came of yore from the kingdom of Britain. And he was king over many

54

other islands, Denmark and Galloway and the Rinns, and Anglesey, and Gwynedd, where Olaf built a strong castle whose mound and ditch are still visible, and which was called the castle of king Olaf. In Welsh, however, it is called Bon-y-Dom. Furthermore, Olaf was son of king Sitric, son of Olaf king of Cuaran, son of Sitric, son of king Olaf, son of king Haarfager, son of the king of Denmark.

[Harald Haarfager and his brothers]
Be it known that Harald Haarfager and his two brothers were sons of the king of Llychlyn. And Alyn his brother was the most hallowed and renowned in all Denmark, whom the leader Thur killed in battle. And while the latter was stripping him and taking a large torque of gold from around his neck, which kings and nobles used to wear of yore, his hands clung to the torque and his knees to his belly. And that was the first miracle which God wrought for him. From then on all the Danes acknowledged him as a saint, and honoured him from that day forth. Many churches were built in his name and in his honour in Denmark, and the sailors call on him especially, and sacrifice to him and offer him many gifts when they are in danger at sea. The leader who killed him was called from that deed forth Thurkiaul, because he had killed the guiltless king.

And be it known that three brothers of him mentioned above voyaged by sea in search of warfare with a royal fleet. At last, they came together as far as Ireland. Harald Haarfager, however, had before then voyaged with a large host, and encircled all Ireland with cruelty, killing its people and putting them to flight, and subduing them throughout its length and breadth. He also built the city of Dublin and many other cities and castles and strongholds, and thus strengthened and consolidated the kingdom all around him. He placed one of his brothers in one of the cities he had built, which was called in their language Porthlairge; and his descendants have been kings of that city since then till today. However, Harald ruled over all Ireland and the Islands of Denmark, - which are in the sea opposite the end of the island of Britain, as the Cyclades lie between the Tyrrhenian Sea and Denmark.

The third brother, namely Rodulf, voyaged with his fleet to France, where he settled and overcame the French through warfare, and subdued a large part of France which is now called Normandy, because the men of Norway inhabit it; they are a people from Llychlyn. And that land was divided into twelve parts, according to the barons and leaders who came first to the part of France called Brittany, or Llydaw. They built many cities there: Rodum, from king Rodulf its founder, which was named as Rome from Romulus, and Remys from Remus; and many other cities and castles and strongholds did he build. From him came the Norman kings who subdued England in battle, namely king William and his two sons, who succeeded him, William of the Long Sword, and Henry and Stephen his nephew, who were contemporaries of king Gruffudd.

Such was king Gruffudd's pedigree on his mother's side, according to his mother's father.

[His pedigree on his grandmother's side]
Again, as regards his grandmother, namely his

56

mother's mother: king Gruffudd was son of Ragnailt, daughter of Mailcorcre, daughter of Dunlang, son of Tuathal, king of Leinster, a fifth part of Ireland. Moreover, Slani, mother of king Olaf, was daughter of Brian, king of Munster, two parts of Ireland. And then Gormflaith was mother of king Sitric; she was daughter of Murchadh, king of Leinster. And she had three famous sons, namely Donnchadh, king of Munster, Sitric, king of the city of Dublin, and Maelsechlainn, king of Meath. Maelmorda, moreover, was son of that queen by Murchadh, king of Leinster.

King Gruffudd had two brothers by the one mother, kings of Ulster. One was Ragnhidr, son of Mathgamhain, who gained two parts of Ireland in a fortnight and a month through his prowess. He was a wondrous leaper; there was not from among all the Irish anyone who could oppose or match him in his leap. His horse also excelled in various feats of speed; Islimach was its name: equal was their leap, his and that of his horse. It most closely resembled Cinnar, the horse of Achilles, and Bucephalus, the horse of the emperor Alexander. Gruffudd's other brother was Aed mac Mathgama, king of Ulster.

[His pedigree in relation to God]
Since the pedigree and kinsmen of king Gruffudd in relation to the world have been enumerated, let us now enumerate his pedigree in relation to God; as the saintly father says of his pedigree and the pedigree of every man in an exposition he gave of this verse from the Psalter: 'Ye are gods, and sons of the Most High are ye all.' Therefore, Gruffudd was son of Cynan, son of Adam, son of God.

57

[Myrddin's prophecy]

Therefore, king Gruffudd having been commended by reason of his worldly and godly pedigree, let us now proceed to the prophecy of Myrddin, bard of the Britons, concerning him. Myrddin prophesied to us about him in this way:

A fierce attacker is prophesied
Who will come intent on onslaught from across the sea.
Despoiler is his name, he will despoil many.

Which reads in Latin: *Saltus ferinus praesagitur uenturus de mari insidiaturus cuius nomen corruptor, quia multos corrumpet.*

O most beloved brethren of Wales, king Gruffudd is greatly to be commemorated, he whom his worldly pedigree and Merlin's prophecy commend in this way. And since that has been done, let us proceed with haste to his own deeds, as they were left to us from an old account. And may Christ be our author and sustainer to this end, and not Diana or Apollo.

[His youth]

Therefore, when Gruffudd was still a lad of good manners and sumptuous upbringing, ascending the years of his youth in his mother's home, and moving among her people, during that time his mother used to tell him every day who and what kind of man his father was, what patrimony belonged to him, what kind of kingdom, and what kind of oppressors were inhabiting it. And when he heard that, he took it greatly to heart and was sad for many days. He, therefore, travelled to the court of king Murchadh, and complained to him chiefly, but also to the other kings of Ireland, that foreign peoples were lords over his paternal

58

kingdom, and he earnestly besought them to help him to seek his patrimony. They took pity on him, and promised to help him when the time should come. And when he heard the answer, he was happy, and gave thanks for it to God and to them.

[He sails for Gwynedd]

Forthwith he embarked in a ship, raised sails to the wind, voyaged by sea towards Wales, and arrived at the harbour of Abermenai. At that time there were ruling over all Gwynedd unjustly and contrary to right Trahaearn son of Caradog and Cynwrig son of Rhiwallon, a petty king of Powys, and they had divided it between them.

Then Gruffudd sent messengers to the men of Anglesey and Arfon, and the three sons of Merwydd of Llŷn, Asser, Meirion and Gwgon, and other leading men to ask them to come in haste to talk to him. And without delay they came and greeted him, and told him, 'your coming is welcome.' Then he besought them with all his might to help him to obtain his patrimony, because he was their rightful lord, and in conjunction with him to repel fiercely with arms their usurping lords who had come from elsewhere.

When the meeting was over and the council dispersed, he again voyaged by sea towards the castle of Rhuddlan to Robert of Rhuddlan, a renowned, valiant baron of strength, a nephew of Hugh earl of Chester, and he besought him for help against his enemies who were in possession of his patrimony. And when Robert heard who he was, and for what he had come, and what his request was, he promised to support him.

[The prophecy of Tangwystl]

And at that time there came a wise woman, named Tangwystl, a kinswoman of his, the wife of Llywarch Olbwch, to greet Gruffudd her kinsman, and to prophesy that he would be king in the future, and to give him the thinnest and finest shirt and a tunic made from the mantle of king Gruffudd, son of king Llywelyn, son of Seisyll: because her husband Llywarch was the most trusted chamberlain and treasurer of Gruffudd, son of Llywelyn.

[Gwynedd subdued]

Then Gruffudd embarked in his ship, and returned by sea to Abermenai.

He sent the fighting men of the sons of Merwydd, who were in sanctuary in Clynnog for fear of the men of Powys who were threatening them, and other noblemen of their kin, and sixty chosen men of Tegeingl from the territory of the Robert mentioned above, and eighty men from Anglesey, to the cantref of Llŷn, to fight with the petty king Cynwrig, their oppressor. Then they proceeded with stratagem, fell upon him without warning, and killed him and many of his men.

Gruffudd was then in Abermenai, namely the harbour mentioned above, awaiting what fate should befall them. There came on ahead in a hurry a young man from Arfon, named Einion, first to give good news, namely that his oppressor had been killed, and to ask as a special boon a comely woman named Delat, formerly a concubine of king Bleddyn, as of yore some youth, son of a man from Amalech, had come running to David to the land of the Philistines from the battle which had taken place on the mount of Gilboa, bearing the sceptre and bracelet of king Saul: and

60

David gave him the bracelet gladly as a reward for the joyful news.

Then there came back with victory the company which had been sent on the expedition. And straightway they urged him to go ahead from that good omen to subdue Anglesey and Arfon and Llŷn and the cantrefs bordering on England, to receive homage from their people. And he proceeded thus and encircled all Gwynedd, his true patrimony, which God had delivered into their hands through His mercy.

And when all those things had been done, urged by them he took a large host towards the cantref of Meirionnydd, where Trahaearn his other oppressor was opposing him. And there was a battle between them in a narrow glen, the place called in Welsh Gwaed Erw, or the Bloody Field, because of the battle which took place there. God gave victory over his enemies that day, and many thousands fell on Trahaearn's side; and hardly did he escape mournfully, and a few with him, from the battle. Gruffudd and his retinue pursued him over plains and mountains as far as the borders of his own land.

Because of that Gruffudd was exalted from that day forth, and deservedly acclaimed king of Gwynedd. He rejoiced like a champion running his course, freeing Gwynedd from the masters who had come to it from elsewhere, and who were ruling it without right, as Judas Maccabeus defended the land of Israel from pagan kings and neighbouring peoples, who frequently made inroads among them. And after everything had been done thus, Gruffudd began to settle his kingdom and organize its people, and rule them with an iron rod gloriously in the Lord.

[An attack on Rhuddlan castle]

After a little time had then elapsed, urged by the leading men of the land, he mustered a large host and advanced towards the castle of Rhuddlan to fight with Robert the castellan, and with the other fierce knights from France who had lately come to England, and had subsequently come to rule the confines of Gwynedd. After he had prepared for battle and raised his ensigns, he plundered the bailey and burned it and took much booty. Many of the mailed and helmeted knights of the French fell from their horses in fighting, and many footsoldiers, and hardly did a few of them escape into the tower. When the king of Ireland and his barons heard that things had happened so successfully for Gruffudd, their kinsman and foster-son, they rejoiced greatly.

[The battle of Bron-yr-erw]

And then the three sons of Merwydd and all the men of Llŷn united against Gruffudd their rightful lord, and killed by night in their lodgings in the country of the Irish fifty-two of Gruffudd's knights and his guard. When Trahaearn heard that, defeated and in flight, he rejoiced that such disunity should have arisen between Gruffudd and his men. Straightway he went to the men of Powys, and urged them to come with him against Gwynedd with a multitude of forces to avenge on them Cynwrig his kinsman. Thereupon there came Gwrgenau son of Seisyll, the king of Powys and his force, and Trahaearn and his force, with one mind determined to subdue the kingdom of king Gruffudd. When the three sons of Merwydd and the men of Llŷn and Eifionydd heard that, they betrayed king Gruffudd, their rightful lord, like perjured, faithless men, and assisted their enemies, serving as their guides to the territory. Two brothers from Anglesey, Tudur and Gollwyn, did likewise, after having received their reward in Clynnog Fawr from Gruffudd.

And when Gruffudd heard of the treachery and alliance against him by his own men together with his enemies, he proceeded against them, and with him the men of Anglesey and Arfon and a few of the men of Denmark and the Irish, and a mighty battle ensued. There was great slaughter on both sides, many fell from the host of king Gruffudd, and many were captured in the battle - Cerit his foster-father, and Mac Ruaidri, the leader of the Irish and lord of Cruach Brendain (that place was the very high mountain of Saint Brendan, a wondrous hermit, surrounded by nine cantrefs). And of the foremost men of Anglesey there fell seventy. King Gruffudd, however, was seated on his horse in the midst of his army, with his flashing sword mowing down both his traitors and enemies, like Agamemnon, king of Phrygia, of yore fighting Troy. And then there attacked Gruffudd Tudur, a youth from Anglesey, the arch-traitor, brandishing a spear, and he turned aside to attack him behind his saddle-bow. When Gwyncu, a baron from Anglesey, saw that, he took him against his will from the battle to his ship, which was in Abermenai. And then they went to the island of Adron, namely the island of the seals. Then they voyaged to Wexford in Ireland. That encounter from then till today is called Bron-yr-erw, or Erw-yr-allt from then till today.

Let not the people, however. be surprised that there is sometimes victory and sometimes defeat for the leaders according to chance, because there has been treachery from the beginning. In

63

that way behaved the people of Israel, who betrayed and delivered their rightful king and their lord, namely Judas Maccabeus, to Demetrius faithless king; nevertheless he, as a warrior of God, like unto a giant and a lion, avenged himself well on both sides. Julius Caesar, the emperor of Rome, after he had conquered the whole world and had pacified it by means of battles, the senators of Rome treacherously killed him with pointed spears in the Roman Capitol. Also Arthur, the king of kings of the isle of Britain and a renowned, famous hero, fought twelve notable battles against the English and the Picts, in the first of which he was defeated and became a fugitive because of treachery in Caer Lwytcoet, namely 'the city of the grey grove *(llwyn llwyt).'* But in other encounters he was victorious, and though an old man, he paid the English and the Picts his oppressors fit retribution in return.

[Another expedition]

After Gruffudd had come to Ireland, he complained bitterly to the king and his chieftains because of his traitors and oppressors. And they for their part found that intolerable, and urged him to return quickly by sea with a fleet equipped with necessities and fighting men. He, therefore, returned to his land cleaving the deep seas with thirty ships full of Irishmen and men of Denmark; and it was in Abermenai they disembarked. Then they found Trahaearn ruling in the land.

And when Trahaearn heard that the royal fleet had come, he was saddened and sighed, and terror and fear struck him. He moved unto himself the men of Llŷn and Ardudwy and their possessions, as many of them as he found, as far as the cantref of Meirionnydd. Gruffudd also and his host took the other part from Llŷn and Arfon to Anglesey, so that they could there be safe under his protection.

Then his Danes, the men of his household and his own family were angered, because they were not getting what they were accustomed to, as had been promised them. And through plunder they took most of Anglesey by force from him, and returned to their land with their ships full of men and riches, and took him also with them, but against his will. Not less then for Gruffudd was the treachery of his Danes than that of his Welsh.

[The Normans ravage Gwynedd]
Then there grew much evil and grief in Gwynedd. And during that time, after a little while, Hugh earl of Chester and many other leaders, namely Robert of Rhuddlan and Guarine of Shrewsbury, and Walter earl of Hereford, mustered the largest host ever of horsemen and footsoldiers. And they brought with them Gwrgenau son of Seisyll and the men of Powys, and traversed the mountains till they came to Llŷn. In that cantref they encamped for a week, causing destruction there daily and ravaging it and inflicting a great slaughter of corpses which they left behind. The land then remained desolate for eight years, and the people of that land were scattered over the world despised and destitute. Many of them went into exile to other lands over many years, and hardly did any of them return to their land. And that was the first plague and fierce advent of the Normans first to the land of Gwynedd, after their advent to England.

[An alliance with Rhys ap Tewdwr]

During that time, after Gruffudd had been for years in Ireland, as guest of king Diarmaid, and with the other leading men, he at last assembled a royal fleet from Waterford which the king had given him, full of Danes and Irish and Britons. And after spreading sails at sea, with the wind favourable behind them, and the sea tranquil, he came to Porth Clais near the archbishop's house of Mynyw.

Then Rhys ap Tewdwr, king of the Deheubarth of Wales, and the bishop and his teachers and the whole community of the lord David and that of the church of Mynyw, came to the harbour. And Rhys first conversed thus with the lord Gruffudd: 'Hail Gruffudd, king of the kings of Wales! To thee am I fleeing. Before thee do I fall on my knees to ask for thy help and strength.' 'Who art thou,' said Gruffudd, 'and for what hast thou come hither?' 'I am Rhys,' said he, 'son of Tewdwr, lord of this territory shortly before now. And at this hour, driven out and put to flight and almost vanished, I am concealing myself in this refuge.' 'Who put thee to flight?' said Gruffudd. 'Lord,' said he, 'three kings from the chief lands of Wales and their hosts lately descended upon my country, and daily they are plundering it.' 'Who,' said Gruffudd, 'are the kings who march through thy men and thy territory so equipped for battle as that?' 'Caradog, son of Gruffudd,' said he, 'from Gwent Uch Coed and Is Coed, and with him his men of Gwent, the men of Morgannwg, and many Norman cross-bowmen; Meilyr son of Rhiwallon with his men of Powys, king Trahaearn and the men of Arwystli.'

And when Gruffudd heard the name of his oppressors, he snorted with rage and asked him what he would give for fighting on his behalf against those men. 'Indeed,' said Rhys, 'half my territory will I give thee, and besides I will do thee homage.' Gruffudd agreed with that. And after that meeting, they proceeded together to the church of David in prayer. And there they became faithful allies through the pledge over his relics.

[The battle of Mynydd Carn]

After they had entered into an alliance in that place, and had received the blessing of the bishop, Gruffudd marched on that selfsame day, with his Danes and Irish and many of the men of Gwynedd to the number of a hundred and sixty, with Cynddelw son of Conus of Anglesey at their head. Rhys for his part and a few Deheuwyr marched with them, happy in his heart because of the help he was getting.

After they had marched a full day's journey, towards evening they came to a mountain, where lay the camps of the kings mentioned above. Then Rhys told king Gruffudd: 'Lord,' said he, 'let us postpone the battle till tomorrow, because it is now evening, and the day is spent.' 'You postpone it,' said Gruffudd with a sigh, 'if that is what you want. I and my army will rush at them.' And so it happened. The kings were however terrified, as they saw the various triumphant forces and the armies of king Gruffudd and his ensigns opposing them, the men of Denmark with their two-edged axes, the Irish with their lances and their sharp-edged iron balls, and the men of Gwynedd armed with spears and shields.

Gruffudd was the first fighter to go into battle like a giant and a lion, without respite scattering his opponents with a flashing sword. He instilled

67

vigour into his men to engage in conflict with their enemies bravely, so that they should not show them their backs in any manner. Then there was a battle greatly to be remembered by the descendants after their forbears. The shouts of the combatants were raised to the sky: the earth resounded with the tumult of horses and foot-soldiers: the sound of conflict was heard from afar: the clash of arms sounded often: the men of Gruffudd fiercely putting on the pressure, and their enemies submitting to them: the sweat of their toil and the blood forming running streams. Amidst that Trahaearn was stabbed in his bowels, until he was on the ground breathing his last, chewing with his teeth the fresh herbs and groping on top of his arms: and Gwcharki the Irishman made bacon of him as of a pig. And in that place there fell around him of his own guard twenty five horsemen. Some others of them were killed in the front troop. Many thousands of them were killed, and the others showed their backs to Gruffudd's men, and turned in flight. Gruffudd for his part, according to his usual practice, victoriously pursued them with his force through the woods and glens, marshes and mountains throughout the night by moonlight, and throughout the following day. And hardly did any of them escape from the battle to their own land.

After the battle was over, Rhys feared treachery on the part of Gruffudd. He withdrew secretly at dusk from the presence of Gruffudd and his men, and did not appear to any of them from then on. Because of that Gruffudd sulked, and ordered his men to ravage the territory of Rhys. And so it happened.

However, the mountain on which the battle was fought the people of the land call Mynydd Carn, namely the mountain of the cairn; because there is a huge cairn of stones under which a hero was buried formerly in olden times.

And after causing a great deal of havoc there and many ravages, Gruffudd marched towards Arwystli and destroyed and killed its people; he burned its houses, and took its women and maidens captive. Thus did he pay like for like to Trahaearn. Then he proceeded to Powys, where he straightway displayed his cruelty to his adversaries according to the manner of a victor; and he spared not even the churches. After he had thus killed his enemies and destroyed their land completely, he returned to his own proper possession and patrimony to rule and pacify it. And there was rest and peace in Gwynedd for a few days.

[The imprisonment of Gruffudd]

And as he was thus enjoying the use of his kingdom, Meirion Goch, his own baron, was stirred by the devil's arrow, accused him before Hugh earl of Chester, and betrayed him in this way. He arranged that the two earls from France, namely the Hugh mentioned above and Hugh earl of Shrewsbury, the son of Roger Montgomery, should come, along with a multitude of footsoldiers, as far as Y Rug in Edeirnion. The traitor then betrayed him with these words: 'Lord,' said he, 'two earls from the border greet thee and beseech thee to come safely with thy foreigners to talk to them as far as Y Rug in Edeirnion.' Gruffudd, believing these words, came as far as the place of his tenancy. And when the earls saw him, they captured both him and his retinue, and put him in the gaol of Chester, the worst of prisons, with shackles upon him, for twelve years. His foreigners, after they had been caught, had the

69

thumb of the right hand of each of them cut off, and in that condition they let them go. And when that was heard, the others dispersed; for the Holy Word says: 'I will smite the shepherd, and the sheep of the flock shall be scattered.'

[His person]

Gruffudd's special acquaintances used to say that he was a man of moderate stature, with yellow hair, a lively brain and round face, of good colour, and large fine eyes, fair eyebrows and fine beard, with round neck, white skin, strong limbs, long fingers, straight legs, comely feet. He was clever and eloquent in several languages. He was also noble, and merciful towards his people, cruel towards his enemies, and most ferocious in battle.

[Earl Hugh in Gwynedd]

And straightway after he had been captured, earl Hugh came to his territory with a multitude of forces, and built castles and strongholds after the manner of the French, and became lord over the land. He built a castle in Anglesey, and another in Arfon in the old fort of the emperor Constantine son of Constans the Great. He built another in Bangor and another in Meirionnydd. And he placed in them horsemen and archers on foot, and they did so much damage as had never been done since the beginning of the world. And the cry of the people ascended unto the Lord, and He listened to them.

[He escapes from prison: reaches Ireland]

In the meantime there had gone by sixteen years, when Gruffudd was released from his prison. For a young man from Edeirnion (his name was

Cynwrig Hir) came to Chester, and a few companions with him, to buy their necessities. And when he saw him in shackles in the city square, he took him on his back and bore him away unnoticed. He went away with his companions in the afternoon, when the burgesses were eating, and provided for him in his own house for a period of days secretly. And after some days when Gruffudd had gained strength, he took him by night as far as Anglesey, where Sanddef son of Aere supported him in hiding.

Then, after a few days, he embarked in a ship with the intention of going to Ireland. However, a contrary wind took them as far as Porth Hoddni in Deheubarth. Then he came ashore with nine chosen companions, and one of them was killed immediately. The people of that land fought with him three times a day, and those three times he overcame them, he and his eight companions; and he himself killed one of the highest born youths who belonged to that territory. Thus did he escape from them. Then continuing on that voyage, he came as far as Ardudwy, doubtful as to what place he should make for because of the treachery of the French. And when the sons of Gollwyn, Eginir, Gellan, Merwydd, Ednyfed, saw him, they took pity on him, and supported him secretly in desolate caves. After some months there joined him a hundred and sixty men, and they wandered from place to place in Gwynedd, inflicting losses in the time of earl Hugh, like king David, son of Jesse, of Bethlehem in the land of Judea, in the time of king Saul. And after the French who were then in the castles saw him causing disorder thus, both they and the people of the land pursued them in wood and open field, like stag-hounds hunting and pursuing a tired stag.

71

When he realised he could not thus escape, he went into the skiff of the canons in Aberdaron, and in it he rowed as far as Ireland. From there again in a month's time he returned in the same skiff, and reached the mouth of the same river whence he had set forth. And from there he voyaged again back to Ireland.

[He regains Gwynedd]

From there, after taking advice, he voyaged by sail and oar as far as the islands of Denmark to king Godfrey his ally, to ask of him ships and their equipment and gear, for then had he first come to him confidently to seek help. And he assisted him enduring and suffering with him in his many perils.

Then Gruffudd voyaged with sixty ships and came to Anglesey, intending in conjunction with the men of the islands to fight against the castle of the French. But the men of the land proved to be too much of an obstacle to them. Then there was a battle ferocious, cruel, intense from morning till afternoon, and many fell on both sides, the bravest men first. And in the midst of that Gruffudd leaped forward in the front troop to cut down the mailed and helmeted French with his double-edged axe, like king David amidst the Phillistines. And the night halted the battle.

After the battle was over, the ships sailed to the islands. He, however, with one ship remained in the island of Ron, namely the island of the seals, plundered a ship coming from Chester, and killed its crew. And on the following day he sailed towards Llŷn, and came to the harbour of Nefyn. When the men of those cantrefs heard that, there came in haste to him the men of Llŷn and Eifionydd and Ardudwy and Rhos and Dyffryn

72

Clwyd, and received him as befitted their rightful lord. After Gruffudd had been fortified with a large host around him through the power of God, he surrounded the castle mentioned above, which was in Anglesey, and fought against it for a period of days, with the French from their forts and strongholds and towers aiming blows and arrows from quarrels and slings and mangonals in showers. Yet they were defeated by the daily fighting of the Welsh. Their court-steward, who was in charge of the castle, was killed and with him a hundred and twenty-four horsemen.

After the castle had been burned and the enemies defeated, Gruffudd rejoiced and moved against the other castles which were at other places in his kingdom, fought with them, burned them, wrecked them, and killed their occupants everywhere. He freed Gwynedd of its castles, took his country for himself, and duly requited his adversaries. And there was peace in Gwynedd for two years.

Remember this also: when Gruffudd was fighting against the castle of Aberlleiniog in Anglesey, with a hundred and twenty men and fourteen youths, he burned it and plundered it and killed many of its men; and after it had been despoiled completely, he returned to the other side of Anglesey where he had three ships. And the men of the castle and of Anglesey pursued him throughout the day, engaging in battle after him fiercely. But they, nevertheless, travelled back with the booty, with French and English in fetters and captive, and many of their pursuers they killed in the long battle. Then fell Gellan harpist and chief poet on the side of Gruffudd in the fleet.

What man, however knowledgeable and brilliant he might be, could relate in full Gruffudd's en-

73

counters and wars between Wales and Ireland and the isles of Denmark and several other peoples. I admit that I can not, and could not, do it, were I as eloquent as the bard Tullius in prose, and the bard Maro in verse.

[His wife and children]

And as Gruffudd thus at times found the path of life smooth, and at other times rough, he took a wife, namely Angharad, daughter of Owain son of Edwin, who according to the testimony of the country's wise men was noble, handsome, with fair hair, large eyes, of fine form, of hawk-like body, and powerful limbs, well-formed legs, the best feet, long fingers and thin nails; genial and eloquent, and lavish with food and drink, and wise and sensible, a woman of good counsel, merciful towards her country, charitable to the needy, and law-abiding in everything.

By her he had sons and daughters. The names of his sons were Cadwallon, and Owain and Cadwaladr; and his daughters were Gwenllian, and Maryret, and Rainillt, and Susanna and Annest. He had sons and daughters also by concubines.

[The expedition of William Rufus]

When William of the Long Sword, king of England, heard of the prowess of Gruffudd and his ferocity and cruelty against the French, he found it intolerable. And he roused his whole kingdom against him, and came as far as Gwynedd with an abundance of troops of horsemen and footsoldiers, prepared to exterminate and destroy all the people completely so that there would not be alive as much as a dog. He had also intended to cut down all the woods and groves, so that there would not be shelter or protection for the people

74

of Gwynedd from then on. And he, therefore, set up camp and pitched his tents first in Mur Castell, with some of the Welsh as his guides. When Gruffudd heard that, he also mustered the host of all his kingdom, and marched against him, in order to prepare ambushes for him, in narrow places when he should come down the mountain. And he became frightened of that, and took his host back through the middle of the land till he came to Chester, without inflicting any kind of loss on that journey to the people of the land. He did not obtain any kind of profit or gain, except for one cow; and he lost a great part of his horsemen and esquires and servants and horses, and many other possessions. Thus did he (Gruffudd) completely avenge the presumption of the French.

Throughout that time, Gruffudd constantly engaged them, sometimes in front, sometimes behind, sometimes to the right, sometimes to the left of them, lest they should cause any kind of loss in the territory. And had Gruffudd allowed his men to mingle with them in the woods, that would have been the last day for the king of England and his Frenchmen. He, however, spared them, as king David of yore spared Saul.

[The expedition of the earls]

After that was over, Hugh earl of Chester, he who was mentioned above, the root of all the evil like Antiochus of yore, mustered a fleet and a mighty wondrous host for the land, with sadness and moaning, and grief, remembering the men of his castle, the razing of his castles and the slaughter of his horsemen. And the other Hugh, earl of Shrewsbury, and his host also, joined with him, that they should come together of one accord to avenge the losses which Gruffudd had inflicted on them. Therefore, they voyaged with their host in their fleet by sea as far as Gruffudd's territory, with Owain son of Edwin and Uchtryd his brother and their force ahead of them. And when that became known, the men of Gwynedd and Powys united to oppose them and not submit. Therefore, the lords of Powys, namely Cadwgan and Maredudd his brother, moved, taking their abodes with them to Gruffudd.

Then after taking counsel together, they went to Anglesey, both they and Gruffudd, and there they defended themselves as in a fortress surrounded by the ocean. For to Gruffudd there had come sixteen ships with long keels as a help to him from Ireland, and they were to fight at sea against the earls' fleet. When the earls heard that, they sent messengers to the ships which had come to assist Gruffudd, to ask them to fail him when he should be in the most dire straits, and to come to them in return for all the goods they wanted. And so it happened. After they had believed the deceit of the French, they all poured into the island and broke their pledge to Gruffudd.

And when Gruffudd knew that, he grieved and feared greatly, for he knew not what counsel he should follow against his adversaries the French and the traitor-ships. Then, after he had consulted with Cadwgan ap Bleddyn his son-in-law, they voyaged in a skiff until they came to Ireland, and left their people and possessions to the will of God and His protection, He who is accustomed to assist every man, when he is most hard-pressed, with an unfailing will. And when their people knew that, they turned and fled, concealing themselves and hiding in caves in the earth, and swamps, and woods and groves, and furn-brakes, and wooded-slopes and precipices, and bogs, and desolate parts, and rocks, and in all kinds of other places where they could hide for fear of the Jews, namely the French and other peoples who had come to attack them. For, as the Holy Word says, 'the people fell without a leader.' And without delay, the earls and their hosts pursued them gleefully that day until evening along the length and breadth of the island, ravaging it and killing its people and breaking the limbs of others. And night halted the chase.

[The appearance of king Magnus]

The following day, behold, through the providence of God a royal fleet at hand, appearing without warning. And, when it was seen, the French and Danes, the traitors who had deceived Gruffudd became dejected. As the French were, however, always treacherous, they sent secretly there and then some of the Welsh who were in league with them to the men of the island, to ask them to come in haste to make peace, and to offer them safety; because they feared that the fleeing Welsh would overcome them on the one side, and the royal fleet on the other. And thus it happened. And thus did the French deceive the traitors of the Welsh, beseiged on every side of the island, after the havoc they had wrought, which could be remembered by descendants after their forbears.

[The death of Hugh earl of Shrewsbury]

However, the fleet which they had suddenly seen was owned by the king of Llychlyn, whom God in his mercy had directed to Anglesey, in order to free the people besieged by the foreigners; for they had called on their Lord in their suffering and grief, and God listened to them. After the king had been told through an interpreter what island it was, and who was master,

77

what ravaging had been done, what pursuing, who were the pursuers, he shared their grief, and became angry, and approached the land with three ships. The French however, fearful like women, when they saw that, fought with their corselets on, and sat on their horses as was their wont, and advanced towards the king and the force of three ships. The king and his force fearlessly fought against them, and the French fell down from upon their horses like fruit from fig trees, some dead, some wounded by the missiles of the men of Llychlyn. And the king himself, unruffled from the prow of the ship, hit with an arrow Hugh earl of Shrewsbury in his eye, and he fell a humped back to the ground mortally wounded from his armed horse, beating upon his arms. And from that incident the French turned in flight, and presented their backs to the arrows of the men of Llychlyn. The king and his fleet sailed away from there, for he had come with much power to look at the islands of Britain and Ireland, which are outside the world, as Virgil said that 'the Britons were entirely separated from the whole world.'

[The Normans and the traitors]

Therefore, earl Hugh and others of the French, joyous because of the return of king Magnus, took with them the people of Gwynedd and all their possessions entirely as far as the cantref of Rhos, for fear of the arrival of Gruffudd at any time. And then were counted the cattle and plunder of every owner, which were divided in half, and with the one half he proceeded to Chester.

There, however, were the perjured traitors from among the Danes, who had betrayed Gruffudd, awaiting the promises which Hugh had given them, captives of men and women, of young men and maidens. And he paid them as faithful to unfaithful, where divine providence affirmed; for he had from afar assembled all the hags - toothless, humped, lame, one-eyed, troublesome, feeble, and offered them to them in return for their treachery. When they saw that, they weighed anchor, and made for the deep sea towards Ireland. He who was ruler at that time caused some of them to be maimed, and their limbs broken, and others were expelled ruthlessly from his entire kingdom.

[He makes peace with Hugh, earl of Chester]
And at that time, behold Gruffudd according to his usual practice coming from Ireland, and he found his whole land desolate, its people having gone to another place. He then sent emissaries to earl Hugh, and made peace with him; and in that cantref three townships were given him. And there he spent his life for years in poverty and grief, hoping for the providence of God in time to come.

[He consolidates his position in Gwynedd]
And then after years had gone by, he journeyed to the court of Henry, king of England, who succeeded his brother as king. From him he got good-will, affection and recognition, through the intercession and diplomacy of Hervé, bishop of Bangor. He gave him with peace and affection the cantrefs of Llŷn, and Eifionydd, and Arllechwedd, along with their people and possessions. And straightway, when Gruffudd returned from the court, he brought settled life to those lands, and for it thanked God, who casts down the proud rich from their chair, and elevates the humble in their stead, who makes the needy opulent, who

abases man and elevates him.

However, from then on everything gradually prospered for Gruffudd, for his hope was in the Lord, and there slipped to him daily others from Rhos and their possessions with them, without the consent of the earl of Chester, and his people multiplied. In the following year he proceeded to Anglesey and its people with him and settled it, and then to the other commotes. In that way he got back through strength everything in Gwynedd, as did Maccabeus son of Mattathias of yore in Israel. And he brought all his people from exile in various parts, those who had gone into exile from the pursuit mentioned above, and he increased possessions in Gwynedd joyfully, as happened in the case of the land of Israel and their return from the captivity of Babylon.

[The expeditions of king Henry]

The earl was offended because his territory had been seized and over-run thus without his consent. And when the king of England heard that, it surprised him, and he opened his treasury, and gave abundantly to horsemen and footsoldiers, and brought with him the king of Scotland and the Scots and the men of the South. He thus came to Gruffudd's territory and encamped at Mur Castell. Gruffudd also, from his experience of warfare, encamped against him on the ridges of snow-clad Snowdon. And from there he negotiated with the king, and the king with him, through the space of some days, and they made peace. King Henry then returned to England, and Gruffudd to his territory.

And again after a period of time, king Henry came back with large hosts, and he encamped in the same place as was mentioned above in the mountain, with the intention of uprooting the territory of Gruffudd and destroying it, and killing and exterminating his people with the edge of the sword. When that was heard, after mustering a host, Gruffudd came against him according to his usual practice, and placed his abodes and villeins and the women and sons in the recesses of the mountains of Snowdon, where they did not suffer any danger. Therefore the king feared that he would fall into the hands of Gruffudd from the danger he was in, when he came down from the mountain, and having made peace with him he returned.

O God, the number of times the earls of Chester contrived to oppose Gruffudd, and could not do it. And the number of times the men of Powys, and they could not. And the number of times the men of the deceiver Trahaearn, but they were not able to bring it to fulfilment.

[Peace and prosperity]

And after that Gruffudd governed for many years successfully and powerfully with moderation and peace, and enjoyed neighbourly relations in accord with the kings nearest to him, namely Henry king of England, Murchadh king of Ireland, and the king of the islands of Denmark; and he was known and prominent both in the kingdoms far from him and in those near him. Then every kind of good increased in Gwynedd and the people began to build churches in every part therein, sow woods and plant them, cultivate orchards and gardens, and surround them with fences and ditches, construct walled buildings, and live on the fruits of the earth after the fashion of the men of Rome. Gruffudd also built large churches in his own major courts, and held his courts and

81

feasts always honourably. Furthermore, Gwynedd glittered then with lime-washed churches, like the firmament with the stars.

He ruled the people with an iron rod, securing concord and peace with the kingdoms nearest to him. And he set his sons, while they were still young men, over the cantrefs farthest away from him, to forestall occupation by others and to maintain them like an immovable wall against foreign peoples and those speaking another tongue, should they happen to contemplate rising up anew against him. The other minor kings made for his court and protection, to seek his help and counsel as often as foreign peoples harassed them.

[He retires and distributes his wealth]

In the end, however, Gruffudd became old and lost the sight of his eyes, and he devoted his strength to deeds of mercy. After he had aspired to eternal renown for prowess, he resolved also to go on his own to a secret, secure place, to lead a godly life, and despise all his worldly dominion completely.

However, as his time to go from this world was approaching, he called his sons and made arrangements for his death, as did king Ezechias at another time. Therefore, he divided all his wealth; and his justice will continue for ever and ever. He sent twenty pieces of silver to the church of Christ in Dublin, where he was born and bred, and the same amount to all the main churches of Ireland. And the same to the church of Mynyw, and the same to the monastery of Chester, and the same to the monastery of Shrewsbury, more than that to the church of Bangor, and ten pieces of silver to Holyhead, and the same to Penmon, to Clynnog, to Bardsey, to Meifod, to Llanarmon, to Dineirth, and to many of the other main churches. What he gave to bishop and archdeacon, priests and those in orders and teachers, and to needy Christians, those goods do I commend to the protection of the Holy Spirit, who knows everything and recognizes it.

[Gruffudd's death]

To witness the end of his life, there came the greatest and wisest men of all the territory, David bishop of Bangor, archdeacon Simeon, a man mature in years and wisdom, the prior of the monastery of Chester, and many priests and scholars anointing his body with consecrated oil according to the injunction of the apostle James. His sons also were there during that time and he blessed them and declared what kind of men they would be in the future, like the patriarch Jacob blessing his sons of yore in Egypt. He commanded them to be brave and to resist fiercely their enemies, as he had done in his day. There also was queen Angharad, his wedded wife, and to her he gave half his property, and two land portions, and the harbour of Abermenai. There were his daughters and some of his nephews, and to all of them also he gave part of his property as sustenance for them after his day.

Welshmen and Irishmen and the men of Denmark bewailed the passing of king Gruffudd, like the lamentation of the Jews for Joshua son of Nun. Eighty-two years of age was Gruffudd, and then he died; and in Bangor was he buried in a tomb on the left side of the high altar in the church. And let us pray that his soul may rest in the same, namely in God, along with the souls of other good kings for ever. Amen.

.23. **L.1.** historia hen: *historia*, a Latin word, was apparently used originally for the written Latin life. Cf. hen *gyvarwydyt* (27.31), which seems to refer to the life in its oral form.

L.2. Yago. In 1033 he is referred to in the Brut as being on the throne of Gwynedd after Llywelyn ap Seisyll, who died in 1023. He was killed in 1039, and succeeded by Gruffudd ap Llywelyn (d. 1063).

L.3. Edward: Edward the Confessor, 1042-66.

Terdelach. The Irish king meant was probably Toirrdelbach ua Briain, grandson of Brian Ború. There are references to him in the Irish Chronicles, including the Annals of Tigernach, where it is said that he died in 1086 (*RC* xvii, 418), after having been on the throne for 22 years, in which case he could not have been there when Gruffudd was born (in 1055). The author of this life is very prone to confuse dates, and facts. At no time was there a king who ruled over all Ireland; yet we learn that, 'towards the end of the eleventh century Pope Gregory VII, Lanfranc and Anselm had accorded both Toirrdelbach ua Briain and his son Muirchertach the courtesy of addressing them as "king of Ireland."' (Cf. *Eriu* xxiv, 57).

L.4. Gwyned, originally the land to the west of the river Conway. But at times it comprised also land to the east of the Conway, including the four cantrefs of Rhos, Rhufoniog, Dyffryn Clwyd and Tegeingl, known as Gwynedd Is Conwy or Y Berfeddwlad.

L.5. dinas Dulyn: a Scandinavian settlement dating originally from 836. It is not easy to determine how strong the Scandinavian element there was by the middle of the eleventh century, but it appears to be still quite prominent and powerful. **Ls.5-6. kymvt Columcell.** There were, of course, no commotes in Ireland. This was the land of Columcille, the saint from the sixth century, in which was sited a monastery bearing his name.

L.6. y magwyt. There is here a clear suggestion that Gruffudd was reared at some place other than his natural home. There are references to his foster-mother (23.8), and his foster-father (32.21), and to him as a foster-son (31.23). Gerald the Welshman *(Opera* v. 167-8) speaks of the affection felt towards foster-children and among foster-brothers in Ireland, a closer relationship than that of natural children and parents. According to Dillon and Chadwick *(CR* 101), 'the time of fosterage ended for boys at seventeen, for girls at fourteen, and they returned home.' If so, Gruffudd would have been back home, and with his mother about 1072.

L.7. Svrth Colomcell: *Sord-Choluim-Chille*, Swords, a few miles to the north of Dublin, at this time within the *Fingal*, the area of Scandinavian influence. It contained a monastery, and must have been a place of some importance, a fact of which the author of the *Historia* was doubtless aware.

L.10. Ragnell. In an Irish text *Ban-shenchas* her name occurs as one of the notable women of the world from the beginning, but nowhere is she mentioned as the wife of Cynan or the mother of Gruffudd.

Avloed: Olaf Arnaid, whose death is recorded under 1012. It represents the Norse personal name *Olafr*, of which various forms are found in

86

Welsh. The form found here seems to represent an oral borrowing of some Irish form of the Norse *A'leifr*, *O'lafr*, such as *Amlaib*, *Amhlaeibh*. The latter would yield *Afloef* in Welsh, whence *Afloedd* by dissimilation or the alternation *-f/dd*, seen in *plwyf/plwydd* 'parish.'

L.11. **a phymet rann Ywerdon:** a fifth part of Ireland; 'a province,' in this case Leinster. The Irish word *coiced* means 'fifth' and also 'province.'

L.13. **ac [y traeth]a.** The text requires emendation here, and it is tentatively suggested that the missing words are *y traeth*.

L.16. **Idwal.** There is a reference to his death in the Brut under 996.

Anaraut. He succeeded his father Rhodri in Aberffraw (Anglesey). He died in 916, and was succeeded by his son Idwal Foel.

L.17. **Rodri.** This is Rhodri Mawr, who was king over all Wales except Dyfed, Brycheiniog, Glamorgan and Gwent. His reign was an illustrious one, and regarded as a milestone in the history of the Welsh; it extended from 844 to 878.

Etill, also *Esyllt*; see *LHEB* 709 for a discussion of the various forms. Here she is described as Rhodri's mother, but according to other sources his mother was Nest, sister of Cyngen, the last of the old line of Powys, and daughter of Cadell. Etill (Esyllt) was his grandmother, mother of his father Merfyn.

Cynan o gastell Dindaethwy. In other lists he is made son of Rhodri Molwynog. He may be the Cynan named with Cadwaladr in prophetic poems as the saviour of the Welsh. According to the Brut he died in 816.

Dindaethwy was the name of a commote in south-east Anglesey. It has as its first element *din* 'fort, stronghold,' while *daethwy* is probably the name of a tribe, whose centre may have been *Dinas*, near Plas Cadnant in the parish of Llandysilio.

L.18. **Catwalader Vendigeit** 'Catwaladr the Blessed'. As noted above, he is associated with Cynan in prophetic verse. He seems to have died (in Rome) in 664, and the Chronicle of the Princes or *Brut y Tywysogion* commences with the great plague which happened in his time. He is described as 'the last king that was over the Britons.' From then on 'the Britons lost the crown of kingship, and the Saxons obtained it;' cf. Pen 20[1]1.

Catwallaun. He was king of Gwynedd, who formed an alliance with Penda, king of Mercia, and fought successfully against Edwin, king of Northumbria. He was killed in battle in 634.

L.19. **Catvan.** He is the *Catamanus* commemorated in an inscription in Llangadwaladr in Anglesey; he died c.625.

Run. He is mentioned in the Life of Cadog, where it is said that he was blinded because of the wrong done by some of his men to the saint, when he was on an expedition in the south. But he repented, and his sight was restored; see *VSBG* 74-78.

Maelgun, known as Maelgwn Gwynedd. According to the *Annales Cambriae* he died in 547 from a great pestilence, probably the Yellow Plague which started in Persia in 542 and then swept across Europe. He is one of the five British rulers from the west castigated by the historian Gildas in his *De Excidio et Conquestu Britanniae*. Gildas refers to him as *insularis draco*, which seems to suggest a connection with Anglesey, although there is also a strong tradition linking his court with Degannwy. His name is prominent in history and tradition down to the twelfth century.

L.21. Cuneda vrenhin, often referred to as *Cuneda wledic.* It is recorded of him that he came down with his sons from the region known as Manaw Gododdin in the North towards the end of the fourth century or the beginning of the fifth to Wales, and drove the Irish from British territories with great slaughter. A shadowy figure, he is nevertheless the most prominent name in early Welsh tradition. Many of the saints are regarded as descended from him; he is the ancestor also of several Welsh royal families. He seems to represent a Romanized Briton, as his immediate ancestors and some of his children have Roman names.

L.24. Onnet. Various forms of this difficult and obscure name are attested; cf. *HGVK* 42.

L.25. Beli Mawr, a prominent and important name in the genealogies. It is also mentioned in the Welsh version of Geoffrey of Monmouth (cf. *BD* 20, 44, 55), where it corresponds to *Heli* of the original Latin.

L.26. Mervyn Vrych. According to the Brut he died in 844.

Guryat. There are other instances of this name, but it is difficult to determine whether the same person is represented by them all. Generally, they appear to suggest a connection with Man and the Old North (the north of England and the south of Scotland). The name occurs in a ninth century inscription in the Isle of Man, *Crux Guriat.*

Cf. further *TYP 396.*

P.24. L.1. Llewarch Hen. It appears that he belonged to the second half of the sixth century, and according to the genealogies was a cousin of Urien Rheged. Stories in both verse and prose grew around him, the verse only surviving in englynion from the ninth century. His family is supposed to consist of twenty-four sons. His name and fame later moved to Wales, to Powys in particular. He was drawn into the Arthurian cycle, but he did not acquire prominence in it; cf. *TYP* 432.

L.3. Coel Godebauc, also *Coel Hen,* who is supposed to belong to the early fifth century. Dwnn (*HVW* ii.226) describes him as *brenin holl ynys Prydain* 'king of all the island of Britain.' His renown continued down to the sixteenth century, and he became *Old King Cole,* who was wrongly connected with Colchester.

godebauc was in origin probably an adjective, and may be equated with the first element of *Uoteporix,* who is commemorated in an inscription of the sixth century. *godeb* appears to mean 'retreat, refuge,' and *godebauc* may have originally meant one who could provide refuge.

L.6. Manogan, also *Mynogan.* It has been shown that this represents an artificially created form, which originated with Nennius: *Bellinus filius Minocanni.* Cf. *TYP* 281-2.

L.9. Lyr. This is probably the same as Geoffrey's *Llyr* (Latin *Leir*). He was king of Britain and had three daughters, one of them *Rhagaw = Regat* above. The other *Llyr* was the old Celtic god, Irish *Ler.*

Ls.10-11. Brutus Ysgwyt Ir: *Brutus Viride Scutum* of Geoffrey's *Historia. Ysgwyt* means 'shield,' and *Ir* 'clean, fresh.' Elsewhere we find also *Taryan Las.*

L.12. Brut, the legendary father of the Britons, *Britto* of the *Historia Brittonum.* *Brut* came to be used as a term for the history of the Britons or Welsh: *Brut* y Brenhinedd (the Welsh version of Geoffrey's *Historia),* and *Brut* y Tywysogion (the Chronicle of the Princes).

Brutus is the form used in Brut y Brenhinedd. For the history of his birth, his exile from Rome and his arrival in Britain, and also for an account of his father Siluius, his grandfather Ascanius, his great grandfather Aeneas, who fled from Troy to Italy, cf. *BD* 3-19; and for a much shorter account in *Historia Brittonum,* cf. *EWGT* 6.

L.13. Eneas Ysgwyt Wyn: Aeneas of the White Shield. The poets refer to him and to Dardanus as forbears.

L.19. Adaf, the full form. Later *-f* was dropped, and we have *Ada.* This must have happened early, because in early poetry we have *Adaf* rhyming with *Eua;* cf. *BT* 73.21,22.

L.22. Enys Vanav. It appears that the Scandinavians became interested in Man and settled in it from the middle of the ninth century on; cf. R.H. Kinvig, *A History of the Isle of Man* (Liverpool, 1974). Note the description of Olaf's 'kingdom' given by the *Historia,* a kingdom which includes the Hebrides, Galloway and Man, in addition to Dublin and Leinster. Anglesey and Gwynedd are also included, and it is in no way improbable that some of the Scandinavian kings had their eyes on these parts of Wales. It is known that from the second half of the tenth century kings of Dublin claimed authority over parts of Britain.

L.24. Denmarc, a reference to the Hebrides, as seems likely.

Galwei, Galloway in the south west of Scotland.

L.25. Renneu: the Rinns, an area of rocky land in the shape of two headlands jutting out from the west of Galloway.

L.27. castell Avloed vrenhin. Nothing is known of this castle, but it is not difficult to see why the author of the *Historia* should wish to make mention of it. He was, of course, anxious to link Gruffudd's grandfather on his mother's side with the kingdom of Gwynedd.

L.28. Bon y Dom, doubtless somewhere in Anglesey. Thomas Pennant mentions *Moel y Don*, three miles from the grave of Henry Rowlands, the antiquarian (d.1723) in the parish of *Llanedwen:*

> About three miles from this place is *Moel y Don* ferry. It is said, that *Aeloedd*, king of Dublin, and father to Racwel, mother of Gruffyd ap Cynan, built a castle here, called in old times *Castell Aeloedd Frenin*, but by the country people *Bon y Dom*.

The information volunteered here must have been derived from the *Historia*. Cf. further HGVK 48.

L.29. Sutric vrenhin. The king meant was probably Sitric Silkiskegg 'Silkbeard,' son of Olaf Cuaran and Gormflaith, who reigned in Dublin from 944 till his death in 1042. He was there in 1014 at the time of the battle of Clontarf, and it was during his reign that the diocese of Dublin was established.

Ls.29–30. Avloed, vrenhin Cuaran 'Olaf, king of Cuaran,' a further indication of the author's ignorance. The king meant was Olaf Cuaran.

cuaràn is probably Irish, meaning a 'shoe made of untanned leather, a sock.' Why this name should be attached to Olaf is impossible to determine. Olaf Cuaran was the most renowned and distinguished of the Scandinavian kings of Dublin, who also ruled in Northumbria. He was in conflict with the English king Athelstan, by whom he was defeated in the battle of Brunanburh in 937. He was in Dublin, however, for most of the time, enjoying much renown and power. But eventually he was overcome by the Irish king Maelsechnaill; he went on a pilgrimage to Iona, where he died in 980.

L.30. Sutric. The king meant is probably Sitric Caoch ('Blind' or 'One-eyed'), one of the foremost leaders of the Scandinavians when their onslaughts in Ireland were resumed at the beginning of the tenth century. During 918-9 he was fighting in Dublin and the neighbourhood against the Irish king Niall Glundubh, whom he defeated. But he did not remain long in Dublin, which he was forced to leave. We next find him in Northumbria, where he ruled until his death in 927.

Avloed vrenhin. It is impossible to determine with certainty who is meant. From here on this pedigree becomes quite obscure and unhistorical. **Ls.30-31. Harfagyr vrenhin.** Probably Harald Harfagri; see below.

L.31. m. brenhin Denmarc 'son of the king of Denmark.' *Denmarc* may refer to Denmark, or more probably, as elsewhere, to the Hebrides. Whichever it is, Harald's father was Halfdan the Black, a ruler over the Vestfold territories in Norway. He had no connection either with Denmark or with the Hebrides.

L.32. Harald Harfagyr, Harald Harfagri, a famed and enterprising king in Norway, c.870-945; *harfagri* suggests that he had fair hair.

L.33. Llychlyn, probably Norway here. But Harald's father could at no time be described as king of Norway.

Alyn. He bears a faint resemblance to Olaf, king of Norway from 1016 to 1030, who fought hard against pagan practices in his kingdom. In the end, however, the leaders and farmers rebelled against him, and he was killed in the battle of Stiklestad, near Trondheim. In the *Heimskringla* (H 245-537) special sanctity is attributed to him; he performed wondrous miracles, especially after his death, and was soon recognized as a saint. He belonged to a later period than Harald Harfagri, and could not have been his brother.

P.25. L.2. Thur. This may be reminiscent of the Scandinavian god Thor. It is recorded that Turgeis, the first of the Scandinavian chieftains to campaign and settle in Ireland, sacrificed to him in Dublin, Armagh and Clonmacnois.

L.6. y glynws y dwylav 'his hands clung.' Note other occurrences such as this, in which mischief is done. Cf. Gerald of Wales: 'it happened... that a boy tried to steal some young pigeons from a nest in Saint David's church in Llan-faes. His hand stuck fast to the stone on which he was leaning, this being no doubt a miraculous punishment inflicted by the saint...' (*GW* 83).

L.9. Daenysseit: the men of Denmark, or more probably the men of the isles, more especially the Hebrides.

L.16. Thurkiawl. This seems to represent the Scandinavian name *Thorkell*. Reference may also be made to Thorer Hund. According to Olaf's saga *(H 514-5)* he was one of those who mortally wounded Olaf in the battle of Stiklestad.

L.25. adeilws. The intention of the author here is to show that Harald was the founder of the Scandinavian settlements in Ireland. We learn a great deal about him in the *Heimskringla* (pp.59-95), a chronicle of the kings of Norway by Snorri Sturluson of Iceland (1179-1241). It is said that he went on an expedition to the west, to the Orkneys and Shetlands, to the Hebrides and Man, but there is no evidence that he was ever in Ireland. However, two of his sons, Thorgisl and Frothi, were there, and they are described as having been the first of the Norwegians to occupy Dublin.

L.30. Porth Larg, *Port Lairge* 'Waterford.' The Scandinavians probably settled there during the ninth century, but Irish sources are agreed that attacks were renewed in the tenth. The *Historia* says that *Harald* set one of his brothers over it, but this cannot be accepted. It appears, however, that Waterford was for a time under the rule of the kings of Dublin. Later, in the tenth century, this ceased, but it is likely that the kings of the two cities belonged to the same family.

Ls.31-32. er henne hyt hediv. The author apparently did not know of the expedition of the Normans under Stronghow in 1070, when Waterford was captured.

L.33. enyssed Denmarc, islands to the north and west of Scotland, and also possibly Man, where there were Scandinavian settlements.

L.35. enyssed Ciclade, apparently the Cyclades, islands off the coast of Greece, to the south east.

mor Tyren, the Tyrrhenian Sea, to the west or south west of Italy. The Cyclades, however, should not be described as situated between this sea and 'Denmarc,' whether the latter means Denmark or the islands off the coast of Scotland. This author fails in his geography, as well as in some other subjects.

L.37. Rodulf. The Norman chroniclers call him Rollo. In 911 an agreement was made between king Charles (the Simple) and Rollo, in which the latter promised to be loyal to the king and to defend Normandy against further invasions from outside. Rollo himself was probably Norwegian, although the bulk of his army must have been Danish. That the author of the *Historia* should have made him a brother of Harald shows how anxious he was to associate Gruffudd with the Norman kings, with whom he would thus share a common ancestry.

P.26. L.9. Rodum, Rouen.

L.11. Romulus. It may be that what was meant originally was *Romulus a Remus,* the two names associated with the founding of Rome.

Remys, Rheims.

Remo, apparently an ablative form of the Latin *Remus.*

L.15. Guilim vrenhin, William the Conqueror, who was king of England 1066-87.

L.16. Guilim Gledyf Hir: *Longue Epée* 'Of the long sword,' the epithet used of the son of Rollo, the second duke of Normandy. The person meant here, of course, was William Rufus, the son of the Conqueror, who was on the throne of England, 1087-1100.

Henri, brother of the above, who was king of

England 1100-35.
L.17. Ystyphan, Stephen, who was on the English
throne until 1154. He was Henry's nephew, and
was involved in a struggle for the throne with
Henry's daughter Matilda.
L.25. Vrien: Brian Ború, king of Munster who
later (in 1002) became high-king. He was a resourceful and distinguished leader, who resisted
the progress of the Scandinavians. He is known
as a staunch patron of literature and the arts.
He was killed in the battle of Clontarf (1014), in
which his army was victorious. Opposed to him
and his men was a league consisting of Scandinavians, the forces of Leinster and others including soldiers from Wales! He was an ambitious
monarch who wished to describe himself as
Emperor of the Irish *(Imperator Scottorum).* He
also seems to have been anxious to develop the
feudal system in his country.
L.26. dwy rann o Iwerdon, 'two parts of Ireland.'
The province of Munster had been divided in two.
Gurmlach. Gormflaith, a notorious lady who was
in her time married to more than one man of
distinction, including Brian Ború. It appears that
she and Brian had become estranged by the time
of the battle of Clontarf. She was important
enough to have her death in 1030 recorded in
the Irish chronicles.
L.27. Mwrchath, Murchadh. His father was Finn,
and he belonged to a royal line in Munster. He
died in 972.
L.28. y hvnnw, should be read *y honno* 'to her,'
namely Gormflaith.
L.29. Dunchath, Donnchadh, son of Brian Ború
and Gormflaith. He succeeded Brian as king in

Munster, and died in 1064.

L.30. **Moelchelen,** Maelsechnaill mac Domnaill, king of the northern half of Ireland, who was *ardri* 'high king' for two periods, 980-1002 and 1014-1022. At one time he was Gormflaith's *husband*, but never her son.

Midif, Mide, Meath, which was originally reckoned as one of the five provinces; the name *mide* means 'middle.'

L.31. **Maelmorda,** Maelmordha, king of Leinster. The author of the *Historia* is again in error, for he was Gormflaith's brother, not her son. Like her, he was a child of Murchadh, son of Finn (d.972). He was one of the adversaries of Brian Ború in the battle of Clontarf, in which he also died.

L.33. **deu vroder vnvam** 'two brothers by the same mother'. Nothing is known about them.

L.34. **Wltw,** Ulster.

P.27. **L.1.** **pythewnos a mis,** lit. 'a fortnight and a month.' There are other references to a period of this length, described thus, in Welsh and in Irish.

L.7. **Alexander amperauder,** Alexander the Great (356-323 B.C.), son of Phillip, king of Macedonia.

L.14. **y wers honn** 'this verse,' namely Psalm lxxxii.6.

L.19. **darogan Merdin.** It is clear that Myrddin (Merlin) had acquired much renown by the twelfth century, and it is no surprise to find the author of the *Historia* linking Gruffudd with his prophecy. He is referred to as a prophet and as a poet from an early period. We find his name in the Gododdin (c.600), and much later in the poem Armes Prydein (c.930); vaticinatory verse was also

attributed to him.   On him generally, cf. R.
Bromwich, *TYP* 469-74.   From the twelfth century on there are frequent references to him by
authors outside Wales.

L.20. val hynn 'like this' or 'in this way.' The
prophecy occurs in the form of an *englyn* of the
old style, found in the early poetry. A few features may be noted. First, it contains three lines
10, 8, 8 with a single rhyme. Secondly, the rhyme
is an Irish rhyme, *er el er*, in which the vowels
correspond, but the consonants *(r l r)* vary according to a fixed pattern.   Thirdly, the language
presents features representative of the Old Welsh
(pre-Norman) period.   The form *llycraut*, with
the ending *-aut* for the third sing. present of the
verb (with future meaning), is an example. Finally, the *englyn* contains some difficult forms, more
especially the second line which is here little
better than a guess, hopefully an inspired one!

.28. L11. Mvrchath vrenhin. The king intended may
have been Murchad, son of Diarmait mac Mailna-
mBó, king of Leinster and the *Gaill* or 'Foreigners' (of Dublin in particular) (d.1072). He made
his son Murchad king in Dublin, and it was in
Dublin that he died in 1070.

L.15. tref y dat, his patrimony to which he laid
claim in Gwynedd as son of his father Cynan.
But there is no evidence that Cynan ever ruled
in Gwynedd.

L.21. porth Abermenei, a harbour at the western
end of the Menai straits.

L.22. enwir: *en-* (for *an-*) negative prefix + *gwir*
'right, claim, law.' They had no right, no lawful
claim to govern. This lack of right is emphasized
time and again in the *Historia.* They were ruling

yn erbyn dylyet, contrary to what was rightful and lawful.

L.23. **Trahaearn vab Caradauc**, ruler over the cantref of Arwystli (the country around Llanidloes and Llandinam), which belonged to Powys originally. According to the Brut he became king over Gwynedd in 1075, the year in which Bleddyn ap Cynfyn was killed. He himself was killed in the battle of Mynydd Carn in 1081. Gwladus, daughter of his son Llywarch, was married to Owain Gwynedd.

Kenwric vab Riwallavn, from Maelor in Powys, another outsider who was in some way related to Trahaearn. According to the Brut he was killed by the men of Gwynedd in 1075 *(RB 28)*.

L.24. **Powys**, the north east, extending from near Chester to the southernmost parts of old Montgomeryshire.

L.27. Arvon. See under *Arvon* below.

P.29. L.6. Robert Rudlan: one of the most distinguished leaders of the Normans in North Wales in the seventies and eighties. He was put in charge of the castle which had been built in Rhuddlan on the river Clwyd. The cantref of Tegeingl was in his possession, and for quite a while he caused much grief and harassment to the Welsh to the west of him. He captured the cantrefs of Rhos and Rhufoniog, and about 1080 built a castle in Degannwy at the mouth of the Conway. He seems to have been recognized by the crown as lord over Gwynedd. He was eventually killed in a skirmish with Gruffudd and his men in 1088 (or 1093) under the Great Orme.

L.7. nei 'nephew,' but according to Ordericus *(OV iii.283)* he was Hugh's cousin *(consobrinus)*.

He was, however, a nephew *(nepos)* of another Hugh, namely Hugh de Grentesmaisnil.

Hu yarll Caer 'Hugh earl of Chester,' one of the most powerful Norman leaders in border areas who dominated and terrorized the Welsh for some thirty years. He was a nephew of the Conqueror, who made him earl of Chester in 1071. He died in 1101, unlamented by the Welsh.

L.13. Tangwystyl. Nothing further is known about her, although her name is not unfamiliar.

L.14. Lewarch Olbwch. There are many references to him in the sixteenth and seventeenth centuries, when genealogists and bards traced pedigrees back to him. He is described as the patriarch of one of the fifteen tribes of Gwynedd (Dwnn, *HVW* i.279 ii.178, 302).

Ls.17-18. Gruffud vrenhin: Gruffudd ap Llywelyn, who was king of Gwynedd and a large part of Wales. He was killed in 1063.

Ls.19-20. guas ystavell: chamberlain. He was one of the twenty-four officers of the court, and served as the king's liaison officer between his private quarters or *ystavell* and the hall *(neuadd).* He must have been entrusted with much secret information. He was also responsible for the king's treasury. He was to receive the king's garments after he had finished with them and his bed-clothes, 'his mantle and his tunic and his shirt and trousers and his hose and his shoes' *LHDd* 38; cf also *LIB* 21-22.

L.24. Kelynnavc, Clynnog in Arfon, in the church of St. Beuno.

L.27. Tegeingyl: a cantref in the north-east, roughly conterminous with the old county of Flint. At this time it was in the possession of

101

NOTES (pages 29/30)

Robert of Rhuddlan.
Ls.28-29. **cantref Lleyn.** See under *Lleyn* below.
L.29. **Kenwric vrenhinyn.** Cf. under 28.23 above.
P.30. **L.3.** **Arvon.** See under *Arvon* below.
Einnyavn. Nothing further is known of him.
L.6. **Delat.** No further information about her is available.
L.7. **Bledyn vrenhin,** probably Bleddyn ap Cynfyn. He and his brother Rhiwallon succeeded Gruffudd ap Llywelyn in Gwynedd. Bleddyn ruled for twelve years, and was killed in 1075. He was ardently praised for his virtues as king; cf. *RB* 28-30.
Ls.7-8. **megys y dothoed gynt:** doubtless a reference to events recorded in 1 Sam. xxxi and 2 Sam. i, but the two accounts do not tally. According to 2 Sam. i.10 the youth had lied in saying that it was he who had killed Saul, and David ordered him to be slain at once. This is another shining example of the author of the *Historia* providing an innacurate account, either by accident or design. The Biblical story in its original form did not suit him, and changes had to be made!
L.9. **hyt yn Philistiim.** According to 2 Sam. i.1 David was in Ziklag.
L.17. **Arvon a Lleyn.** See under 41.19 below.
L.18. **cantreuoed kyffinyd y Loegyr:** the cantrefs in the border country, including Tegeingl and other lands occupied by the Normans from Chester, Shrewsbury and Hereford.
Ls.23-24. **cantref Meiryonnyd:** land which extended from the estuary of the Dyfi as far as the estuary of the Mawddach, including the valley of the Wnion.

NOTES (pages 30/31/32)

L.27. Gvaet Erw. Cf. *HW* ii.381 'perhaps the narrow glen now known as Dyffryn Glyncul;' there is no reference to such a battle in the Brut.

Ls.33-34. e wlat e hun: Arwystli and Meirionnydd.

.31. L.3. Iudas Machabeus: the leader of the Jews in their revolt against the oppression of Antiochus Epiphanes, the king of Syria (d.164 B.C.). In 162 B.C. Demetrius was king in Antiochia, and Judas fought against him also. But in 161 he was defeated and killed in an encounter with the enemy, when most of his troops had deserted him.

.32. L.2. Gurgeneu m. Seissyll. He is again mentioned as being in league with the Normans against Gwynedd (34.20). His death is recorded in the Brut under 1081.

Ls.7-8. eu hargluyd priodaur, also 29.1. Note the emphasis by repetition. In the Laws *arglwyd* alternates with *brenhin* (king) to denote the territorial ruler.

L.12. kyuarws 'gift, reward.' It appears that the basic meaning is that of sign, token, indicating some kind of recognition, of respect or honour, and an indication also that the recipient was of lower status than the donor. *kyuarws* was paid by a king, according to the honour of the recipient. In *Kulhwch ac Olwen* Culhwch's father advises him to go to Arthur to have his hair trimmed, *ac erchych hynny yn gyuarws it* 'and ask for that as your reward.' It appears that here *cyfarws* in some way signifies admission as member of the tribe, and as recognition of kinship.

L.14. y brat a'r dvundap 'the treachery and alliance.' Note how the author attributes Gruffudd's lack of success to the treachery of others.

This happens time and again.

L.20. **dalyassant.** This is active and means '(they) captured,' but a passive seems to be required here.

L.21. **Varudri.** This probably represents the Irish *Mac Ruaidri*, but it is not possible to identify the name. He is described as *argluyd Cruc Brenan*, a title which cannot be traced in any Irish source.

L.22. **Cruc Brenan** *Cruach Brendain*, doubtless a reference to the mount of Brendan in the Dingle peninsula in west Kerry, which contained the second highest point in Ireland (3,127 feet). In these parts remain traces of an eremitic establishment linked with the name of Saint Brendan, the noted navigator (484-577 A.D.).

It is likely that there were Scandinavians in the peninsula, connected with the settlement in Limerick, and some from this area may have been in Gruffudd's force.

L.28. **Agamemnon:** a Greek hero, the ablest leader in Greece who led the Greeks in the war against Troy. According to Homer, he was the bravest of the warriors in that war.

L.32. **barwn** 'baron' OF *ber: baron*, E *barun*. There are no early examples of it. It is clear that the translator here is using a term more appropriate to his own time than to that of the *Historia*. It is difficult to guess what could have been in the original Latin; in *BD* 94.3 it occurs for *principis*.

L.35. **enys Adron,** Skerries, near Llanfair-yng-Nghornwy in the north-west of Anglesey. Another name was Ynys y Moelrhoniaid (pl. of *Moelrhon* 'seal;' the rocks there must have reminded someone of seals.

L.36. Llwch Garmavn: Wexford, where there was a Scandinavian settlement dating from the ninth century.

L.37. A'r gyvranc honno 'And that encounter.' The Brut refers to the battle under 1075, but gives no details.

P.33. **L.1. Bronn yr Erv.** It appears that the battle was fought near Clynnog Fawr in Arfon; but cf. *AC* xi (1865), 86: 'But that field is said by old historians to have been near Harlech, and I apprehend can be no other than the spot where the new mansion of Deudraeth Castle now stands, which was formerly called Bronyrerw, just over Traethbach, where the contending factions of the north and south would be likely to meet.'

L.7. dyledawc 'rightful,' the king with *dyled* 'right, claim, entitlement.' This is stressed throughout the *Historia*, Gruffudd's right to his throne in Gwynedd. It was ill-luck and treachery that foiled his attempts to make his ascendancy secure and lasting.

L.8. Demetrius, king of Syria.

L.11. Ulkessar, Julius Caesar. This is the form that obtains in Middle Welsh prose-texts, and among the bards.

L.14. Cabidyldy, 'Capitol, senate-house,' consisting of *Cabidwl* (a learned borrowing from Lat. *capitulum*) + *ty* 'house.'

Arthur. It is difficult to determine whether it is the author's acquaintance with the native Welsh tradition that accounts for this reference to Arthur, or whether it is indicative of his increasing renown at this time generally in circles out-

NOTES (pages 33/34)

side Wales. Cf. F. B. Artz (*The Mind of the Middle Ages* p.348): 'The popularity of Arthur was beginning to grow; by the 13th century he was ranked as one of the 'Nine Worthies,' along with Hector, Alexander, Caesar, Joshua, David, Judas Maccabaeus, Charlemagne, and Godfrey of Bouillon.' Most of these are mentioned in the *Historia*.

L.16. **deudec prif emlad**, a reference to the twelve battles of Arthur mentioned in the *Historia Brittonum* c.56 (early ninth century).

L.17. Fichtyeit, Picts.

e gentaf onadunt. Cf. HB: *primum bellum fuit in ostium fluminis quod dicitur Glein* 'the first battle was at the mouth of the river which is called Glein.' It has been suggested that this battle was fought early, c.496, in Bernicia (in Northumberland) near the place where the river Glen flows into the Till, and was an onslaught against the enemy's main stronghold in Bernicia, *Gefrin* or Yeavering Bell; cf. Tolstoi, *B* xix (1961), 120-2.

Ls.18-19. yg Caer Lwytcoet. The author wants us to believe that Arthur lost this battle ('because of treachery') and was victorious in the others. Here again he seems to be manipulating the information he possessed to serve his own ends.

L.35. mudav 'move.' There are many references to the removal of people and property (mainly cattle) in primitive society.

P.34. L.10. en llavn o deneon. It is clear that capturing and taking people away was one of the more important purposes of plundering expeditions in Wales and elsewhere. It is known that there

106

was a brisk slave trade at this time. Gerald of Wales speaks of much trading in slaves between Ireland and England in the twelfth century, and we have not a few references to plunderers taking people back with them in their ships. Cf. *ONRW* 34-37. In 47.8-11 it is said that the earls at the time of their expedition to Anglesey in 1098 had promised captives to the 'Danes' as a reward for betraying Gruffudd.

L.18. **Gvarin o Amwythic,** one of the foremost men of Roger, earl of Shrewsbury. He must have often been involved in conflicts with the Welsh, but there is evidence that he was dead by 1086.

Guallter yarll Henford. It is wrong to describe him as the earl of Hereford. The person meant is Walter de Lacy, whose position in Hereford was similar to that of Gwarin in Shrewsbury under Roger, and to that of Robert of Rhuddlan under Hugh, earl of Chester. Ordericus (*OV* ii. 218) refers to him as one of the proven soldiers entrusted by the Conqueror with the protection of the border areas against the Welsh.

P.35. **L.1.** **trwydet.** It now means 'licence,' but formerly it denoted permission to stay in court, and receive sustenance and hospitality there.

Diermit Diarmait. It is difficult to determine which of the Diarmaits is meant here.

L.3. **Porthlarc.** Waterford.

L.7. **Porth Cleis,** a mile to the south-west of St. David's, where the river Alun enters the sea. It was here that the Twrch Trwyth landed from Ireland, according to the tale of *Culhwch and Olwen* (*WM* 500. 36-38).

L.8. **archescopty Mynyv** 'the archbishop's house

of Mynyw.' The use of *archescopty* may be indicative of Owain Gwynedd's support for the campaign to have St. David's recognized as a metropolitan see. On the other hand, the use of *archescob* may be purely honorific, with little (if any) significance. It is known that in the forties of the twelfth century Bernard, bishop of St. David's, campaigned for metropolitan recognition for his church, without success, although it appears that he came close to achieving his goal at one stage.

Mynyv, the old name for St. David's. It is the name used in the Brut, where there are frequent references to arson and pillage there between 810 and 1091. Under 1081 it is recorded that the Conqueror visited the church as a pilgrim, but according to other sources, English and Norman, more mundane matters claimed his attention. So the Anglo-Saxon Chronicle s.a.1081: 'In this year the king led levies into Wales, and there freed many hundreds.'

L.9. Rys m. Teudur, king of Deheubarth from 1079 to 1093, when he was killed by the Normans near Brecon. It is probable that he enjoyed much prestige and authority at a time when Gruffudd for the most part led the life of a pirate and plunderer. He may have met the Conqueror at St. David's in 1081 when they entered into an agreement confirming Rhys's position as Lord of Deheubarth. It is interesting to note that according to *Domesday Book* in 1086 some 'Riset de Wales' made to the king a payment of £40 a year. Here it is intriguing to find the *Historia* belittling him as one deficient in power and bravery, and also as one who could not always be trusted (37.19-25).

L.10. Deheubarth Kemry, Dyfed, Ceredigion and Ystrad Tywi.

escob: Sulien, who was there for the second period (1080-5), after the death of Abraham. His first period extended from 1073 to 1078. He came originally from Llanbadarn, but received some of his education in Scottish and Irish schools, possibly in Iona, Glendalough or Clonmacnois. He must have been a scholar and diplomat of distinction, and reared a distinguished family who shared his most illustrious attributes. His son Rhigyfarch composed the Life of St. David, sometime in the late eighties, as appears likely. The Brut records his death under 1091.

L.11. clas, from Lat. *classis.* It was used of the community in the early pre-Norman establishment in Wales.

L.11-12. e borth, for *porthloed* 'harbour.'

L.21. e nodua honn, 'this refuge.' The impression given is that Rhys was in flight, and had come here to seek refuge from his enemies, but this is not stated in the Brut.

L.28. Caradauc m. Gruffud, king of Gwynllwg, and one whose power and authority increased after the death of Gruffudd ap Llywelyn in 1063. He was in conflict with the English and with his fellow-kings in Wales, and was not averse to joining forces with the Normans, if he thought that such an alliance suited his purpose. We find him gradually advancing towards the west; Glamorgan was now under his yoke, and he must have cast covetous eyes on Deheubarth. But the end was near for him, and he was killed in the battle of Mynydd Carn.

Ls.28-29. Gwent Uch Coet ac Is Coet: two cantrefs forming the land of Gwent, which lay between the three rivers, Usk, Wye and Monnow, and the sea. The more southerly of the two and the smaller was Gwent Is Coed. It was also the richer as it contained the strip of land bordering on the Bristol Channel. Between it and Gwent Uch Coed to the north, as the names of the two cantrefs suggest, lay a fairly extensive area of wooded country. To the west lay the cantref of Gwynllwg, between the Usk and Rhymni. After the Act of Union (1536), Gwynllwg and Gwent were joined to form the county of Monmouth. **Gwenhwyssyon,** pl. of *Gwenhwys,* a person (or persons) from Gwent.

Ls.29-30. Morgannvc.   At an early period it was meant to cover the area from Swansea to the river Wye, and included Ewias and Ergyng (Archenfield), now part of Herefordshire. Like Dyfed it consisted of seven cantrefs.

L.30. albryswyr: pl. of *albrysiwr (albrys + iwr);* a borrowing (ME *arblast[e], alblast,* OF *arbaleste).* **Nordmannyeit.** It is known that Caradog was in league with the Normans. They were fighting side by side in the battle on the banks of the Rhymni in 1072, when Maredudd ab Owain, king of Deheubarth, was killed; cf. *RB* 27.

L.31. Meilir m. Riwallaun. The Brut records his death at the battle of Mynydd Carn; cf. *RB* 31.

P.36. L.8. Gwyndit, the men of Gwynedd.

Ls.8-9.   Kendelu m. Conus.   Cf. his pedigree back to Cunedda in *EWGT* 111. Cf. *ibid* 155 re-

garding his son Hwfa: 'The family of Hwfa ap
Cynddelw was associated with the cwmwd of
Llifon, Anglesey. Hwfa was probably born c.1090.'
He was the patriarch of one of the fifteen tribes
of Gwynedd; cf. *TWTP* iii. 428-9.

L.14. **dywededigyon:** pl. of the past participle
passive of *dywed-yt* 'said, spoken, mentioned.'
The frequent use of this participle in translated
works certainly reflects Latin usage.
uchof 1. sing. of the prep.|*uch* 'above,' but here
used as an impersonal adverb. Cf. *uchot,* originally the 2 sing. of the same prep.

L.23. **eu bwyeill deuvinyauc** 'their two-edged
axes.' The sword and axe were common among
the Scandinavians. Cf. *HV* 34: 'Most beloved of
all were the sword and the axe... A single-edged
pointed sword was still in use among the northern
peoples in the ninth century, but the favourite
blade of the Viking period is two-edged and
heavy, with a deep wide fuller.'

L.24. **peleu haearnaul kyllellauc** 'sharp-edged
iron balls.' It is difficult to determine precisely
what these were. Cf. for example O'Curry,
Manners and Customs of the Irish (ed. Sullivan),
i.462-3: 'the Irish suist or war flail, from which
hung iron balls attached to chains.'

L.25. **gleiuyauc:** adj. from *gleif* 'spear,' a borrowing (Fr. *glaive,* also E). Cf. Gerald: 'They
use very long spears in this area. Just as the
bow is the chief weapon in South Wales, so here
in Gwynedd they prefer the spear.' *(GW* 182).

.37. L.27. Menyd Carn. It is difficult to determine
the location of the battle which, nevertheless,
must have been fought somewhere in the south,

and in the west, not far from St. David's. Cf. *HGVK* 78:

> But the fact seems to be that the battle was fought in the dominions of Rhys, where the army was ravaging and at a spot within a day's march of St. David's. The ordnance maps mark near Newport (Pembroke) a *Mynydd Carn Ingle* against numerous other carns. This is a possible site of the battle, since it has the 'carnedd' spoken of in the text, and is about 20 miles from St. David's.

L.32. e kerdus Gruffud parth ac Arwystli. It may be asked whether there is an echo here of Owain Gwynedd's expedition against Arwystli in 1162, an expedition recorded in the Brut; cf. *RB* 143.

P.38. **L.2. y'u briodolder,** to land over which he had proprietory right of *exclusive* occupation. See A. R. William, *Llyfr Iorwerth* (Cardiff, 1960), 46, 47, 50, 55, 56, 58, and cf. *WHR* (Special Number 1963), 41-43; *TC* (1963), 11-13. 'Under Welsh law, continued occupation of land for four generations created *priodolder*. The word suggests a *proper* relation to the land, i.e. *property* or *proprietorship*: cf. *priodas*. From the fourth generation on, the occupier was *priodor* and in legal theory *priodolder* was not lost by non-occupation for nine generations.' *(WLW* 214-5). Note again the emphasis on Gruffudd's absolute right; he is described as eu harglwyd *priodaur*(29.1, 31.26, 32.7-8) while the usurpers from outside are called *ampriodoryon* (29.2).

L.4. dieuoed 'days,' a dual pl. consisting of *dieu* pl. of *dyd* 'day' + a pl. ending -*oed*.

L.6. Meiryaun Goch. He is probably to be ident-

ified with the 'Meiriawn goch o Leyn' named in
'Llwyth Bran' *(EWGT* 115), the Meirion ap Merwydd
(Meurig) ap Tangno, contained in 'Llwyth Gollwyn'
(ibid. 117-8), he and his two brothers Asser and
Gwgawn. The three are named in the *Historia*
(28.27-8); Gruffudd sought help from them on his
first expedition (28.27).

L.7. y varwn e hun 'his own baron.' Cf. Francis
Jones: 'The Anglo-Norman influence is noted in
the description of Meirion the Red as Gruffydd's
baron' TC 1948, 329.

L.10. Hu yarll Amvythic. At this time it was
his father Roger who was earl of Shrewsbury. He
died in 1093, and was succeeded by Hugh. Hugh
died on the expedition to Anglesey in 1098 (p.46).

Ls.10-11. Royzer o gastell Baldwin: Roger Montgomery, who was created earl of Shrewsbury
c. 1071.

L.11. Castell Baldwin, a castle built by Roger.
It was destroyed in 1095.

L.12. y Ruc. *Y Rug* was about a mile and a half
from Corwen. The name consists of the noun
grug 'heather,' which has undergone the soft
mutation after the article ỳ. .

L.13. Edeirnyavn, a commote which was in the
possession of the Normans by 1086. It was here
that the combined forces of the Welsh assembled
to withstand the expedition of Henry II in 1165.

L.16. dieither 'foreign' here, a suggestion that
Gruffudd's force at this time consisted of foreigners (mercenaries from Ireland or the Islands),
rather than Welshmen from Gwynedd.

L.19. daleassant '(they) captured.' According to
the *Historia* he was captured by the earls, but

Ordericus Vitalis in a poem speaks of his being
captured by Robert Rhuddlan; cf. *HGVK* clii.

Ls.21-22. **deudeng blyned** 'twelve years:' but cf.
39.17-18 *vn vlyned ar bemthec* 'sixteen years.'

Ls.22-23. **a dorret y uaut deheu** 'had the thumb
of his right hand cut off,' in order to ensure that
he could not use arms, such as shoot with a bow.

L.26. **Mi a drawaf y bugeil.** Cf. Jesus's words
in the upper room (Mth xxvi.31): 'for it is written,
I will smite the shepherd, and the sheep of the
flock shall be scattered abroad.'

L.27. **y genveint** 'the flock' here, a learned borrowing from the Latin *conventio.*

P.39. L.2. **amravaellyon yeithyoed** 'several languages.'
The possible languages are Welsh, Irish, Norse,
French, English and Latin. It is not likely that
he knew much Latin, and he cannot have been
fluent in all the others. He probably knew Welsh,
and since he must have spent some time with
mercenaries, who spoke a mixture of Norse and
Irish (the *gic-goc*), he can hardly have been un-
acquainted with these languages. He must have
known some French before the end of his days,
but it is not likely that he came into much contact with English.

L.5. **Hu yarll**, the earl of Chester.

L.8. **castell**, probably Aberlleiniog.

L.9. **Arvon:** Caernarfon, or rather Segontium,
the old Roman fort that was built first in 78 AD,
and was finally relinquished by the Romans c.380-
90. But this fort, like other old Roman centres,
continued to attract 'antiquarians' and storytellers
in subsequent periods, and they were linked with
great names in Roman history, such as Constan-

tine, Helena, Maximus; cf. R. S. Loomis, *WAL* 1-18.
Ls.9-10. Custennin amperauder, vab Constans Vaur.
There has been considerable confusion regarding
Custennin (Constantine). Constantine the Great,
the first Christian emperor (307-337 AD) was son
of Constantius and Helena, who was thought to
have discovered the Cross in Jerusalem. She was
confused with Elen Luyddog, the heroine of the
Dream of Macsen Wledig, with the result that
Helen and Constantine became Welsh. Then
Constantine was confused with another of the
same name, who was made emperor in York in
407. He was again confused with Constantine
the Blessed *(BD 85-86),* Custennin Fendigaid.

In *HB* (c.25) there is reference to *Constantius,*
son of *Constantinus Magnus,* and the fifth of the
Roman emperors in this country. It was here in
Britain (or in Wales) that he died, and his tomb is
to be seen near the city called *Cair Segeint,* as
the letters on his tombstone show. *Constantius*
also was the name of the ninth emperor (c.27).
He reigned 'in Britain' for sixteen years, and it
was there he died.

In the Brut of Geoffrey there is a reference to
Constans, who had been sent to Britain to conquer it. After the death of Coel he takes the
crown of the kingdom and also Coel's daughter
Elen *(Elen Luydavc)* as wife. A son was born to
them named Custennyn, who later became emperor of Rome; cf. *BD* 69-70.
Ls.14-16. A llef y bobyl a esgynnvs... Cf. Ex. 2.
23-4: '... and they cried, and their cry came up
unto God by reason of the bondage. And God
heard their groaning,.....'

L.32. **Port̟h Hodni** should be looked for somewhere at the mouth of the Usk in the south-east,
if we have here another version of the incident
recorded in the Life of Gwynllyw (*VSBG* 182-4).
Gruffudd is reported to have been driven from
the confines of Wales by war. He sailed to the
Orkneys, and from there he voyaged southwards
with twenty four ships, full of a spirit of revenge,
and intent on plunder. They reached the mouth
of the Severn, and cast anchor in the estuary of
the Usk. Then they landed and collected much
plunder. The most despicable of all their deeds
was breaking into the church of Gwynllyw, and
ravaging it before returning to their ships. Gruffudd, however, did not take part in such des-
ecration. The ships were wrecked in a storm,
except for two, owned by Gruffudd. Eventually,
he returned and made his peace with king William.
If the same incidents are represented by the two
accounts, they must have occurred before 1087
when William died; and if so, at a time when
Gruffudd according to the *Historia* would be a
prisoner.

It is not easy to identify *Porth Hodni*, *Hodni*
and *Honddu* (by metathesis, seem to be essentially
the same, despite the variation -*i*/-*u*). The river
Honddu flows into the Usk in *Aberhonddu* (Brecon),
but this is too far from the sea. We must also
consider *Llanddewi Nant Hodni* (Llanthony) in
Gwent. It had an abbey which would perhaps
be known to an ecclesiastic from the north, but
a place at the mouth of the Usk would hardly be
called *Porth Hodni*. It is idle to speculate further.
Furthermore, we learn that it is in Deheubarth,

116

which means that it cannot be at the mouth of the Usk; cf. *35.*10n.

.40. L.10. Gollwyn. According to Bartrum *(EWGT* 157), 'Gollwyn was probably born c.1025.' Robert Vaughan of Hengwrt states that Harlech was formerly known as *Caer Gollwyn.* 'Llwyth Gollwyn' was one of the fifteen tribes of Gwynedd. See *EWGT* 117, where the names of his sons and his pedigree are given.

Later, it appears that there was a connection by marriage between the families of Gollwyn and Gruffudd; cf. *EWGT* 118.

L.16. Ysai: Jesse the Bethlehemite; cf. 1 Sam. xvi.1.11.

L.22. Aberdaron, at the extreme end of the Llŷn peninsula, and opposite Bardsey. It is known that there was a church there, to which Gruffudd ap Rhys fled for refuge in 1115; cf. *RB* 85.

L.29. Gothrei vrenhin, Godred Crovan, king of Man and the Isles (c.1080-95), who succeeded in extending his authority as far as Dublin and Leinster. He was born in Iceland, and in 1079 defeated Man and subdued it in the battle of Scacafell. In 1094, when Gruffudd was seeking help from him, he had defeated Muirchertach ua Briain, king of Munster, but later that year he was defeated and driven out of Dublin. The following year he died of a plague.

Ls.33-34. gan gytdiodef ... a'e uenych bergleu ef. There is here a hint that the two had been together before on quite perilous expeditions, and it reinforces the impression gained from other sources that Gruffudd during this period was without a kingdom, enduring the hazards of the pirate and adventurer.

L.35. odena. From here to 42.17 we have the *Historia's* version of the Welsh revolt against the Normans in 1094.

a thriugein llong ganthav 'with sixty ships,' a comparatively large fleet.

P.41. L.2. **castell y Freinc,** probably Aberlleiniog in Penmon, in the south-east of Anglesey.

Ls.9-10. vegys Dauyd vrenhin. Cf. e,g. 2 Sam. v.20, viii.1, xxi.15.

Ls.12-13. y llongeu a gerdassant y'r enyssed. The ships sailed for the Hebrides (or Man). The departure of the ships may well have been caused by Gothrei's troubles, after he had been driven from Dublin.

L.17. porth Nevyn, on the northern side of the peninsula, to the south-west of Abermenai.

L.19. Lleyn: a cantref which comprised the western part of the penninsula. It contained three commotes.

Eiuyonyd ac Arduduy: two commotes which formed the cantref of Dinoding, separated by the Traeth Mawr. Eifionydd lay to the east of Llŷn, between the Erch and the Traeth, and Ardudwy towards the south as far as Barmouth, and inland over desolate and unproductive terrain. In this commote were situated Harlech and Mur Castell. **Arvon:** the cantref to the east of Llŷn, extending as far as the river Cegin betwen Bangor and Llandegái, and down as far as the fastness of Snowdon. On its southern boundary were Eifionydd and Ardudwy.

L.20. Ros: the cantref which lay between the rivers Elwy, Clwyd, Conwy, and the sea, which extended as far as Capel Garmon.

Dyfrynt Cluyt: a rich cantref which consisted of

the southern part of the vale of Clwyd from Bodfari to Derwen.

Note that the author does not mention the cantrefs of Arllechwedd (between Arfon and Rhos), Rhufoniog (between Rhos and the vale of Clwyd) and Tegeingl (to the east).

42. L.9. teir llong, but *one* ship according to 41.3 above. Slip-shod again!

L.16. Gellan telynyaur penkerd. The *penkerd* (*pen* 'chief' + *kerd* 'craft, song') was the chief poet, the leader in a skilled craft, but he could also perform the duties of another bardic officer, namely *y bard teulu* 'the bard of the bodyguard,' who is probably meant here. The poet Dafydd Benfras (c.1220-60) is described as a warrior. It appears that the Normans had their *jongleur* at the battle of Hastings, and a poet accompanied Magnus on his expedition in Anglesey in 1098. It is said in the Laws that 'when the bard of the bodyguard assumes his office he receives a harp from the king, and a gold ring from the queen. And he is never to part with the harp' (cf. *LIB* 22).

L.23. Tullius vard: Marcus Tullius Cicero (106-43 BC), the Roman orator, writer, and statesman. **Maro vard:** Publius Vergilius Maro (70-19 BC), Virgil, the Roman poet.

L.27. Angharat. Her death is recorded in the Brut s.a. 1162.

Ewein vab Edwin. He probably had links with Tegeingl, a cantref now in the possession of the earl of Chester. His mother was Iwerydd, half-sister of Bleddyn ap Cynfyn; cf. RB 100. His father Edwin is described as patriarch of one of the fifteen tribes of Gwynedd; cf. e.g. *TWTP* iii. 444-5. His own death is recorded in the Brut s.a. 1105.

P.43. L.2. Catwallavn: d.1132.

Ewein: Owain Gwynedd, d.1170.

Ls.2-3. Catwalader: d.1172.

L.3. Guenlliant. As Sir J. E. Lloyd showed (*HW* ii.417n), she could not have been a daughter of Angharad, but of one of the concubines. She was the famous wife of Gruffudd ap Rhys ap Tewdwr, who died while leading an assault on Cydweli castle in 1136; cf. Gerald, *GW* 136-7.

L.10. dyuot hyt yg Gwyned. The *Historia* speaks of only one expedition (against Gwynedd), but in other sources two expeditions (in 1095 and 1097) are recounted.

L.17. Mur Castell. No one else mentions Mur Castell in connection with the expeditions of William Rufus, and the author of the *Historia* may well have confused these with the expedition of Henry I in 1114.

L.30. a'e lu ganthunt. An emendation seems required here. A verb is missing, and we should probably read *a'e lu a luydassant ganthunt:* '[Gruffudd] and his host engaged in conflict with them.' *lluydaw* 'to engage in conflict, to muster a host.'

P.44. L.1. Freinc, the name usually used in the *Historia* for the Normans.

a arbedus idav ef 'he spared him.' There is no suggestion of this by anyone else, but the life of Henry I was in danger on one of his expeditions.

L.2. megys Dauyd vrenhin. Cf. 1 Sam. xxiv. 1-8.

L.5. Antiochus: Antiochus Epiphanes, 175-164 BC, king of Syria and the neighbouring countries. It was against his cruel oppression that Judas Maccabaeus rebelled; cf. under 31.3 above.

NOTES (page 44)

L.7. a choffau y gastellwyr... There was much plundering in the territories of the earl of Chester (and also of the earl of Shrewsbury), resulting from the revolt of the Welsh in 1094, and it is likely that he had not until then had the opportunity for revenge and for the re-possession of Gwynedd. He was in Normandy when the revolt broke out in 1094, and he must have been occupied with the affairs of his king for much of the turbulent times of 1095 and 1096. He is known to have been fighting in Normandy in 1097 (*OV* iv.20).

Ls.8-9. Hu arall: the earl of Shrewsbury, after the death of his father Roger in 1093. His territories also suffered as a result of the uprising of the Welsh. In 1095 the castle of Montgomery was destroyed.

L.13. Ewein vab Edwin: Gruffudd's father-in-law; see under 42.27 above. Brenhinoedd y Saesson also states that he was promoting the expedition of the earls: 'And after the French had learnt that, they took Owain ab Edwin at their head to go to Anglesey' *(BS* 91). Later the same year, when the men of Gwynedd rebelled against the oppression of the Normans, it was he who led the revolt: 'And after that, since the men of Gwynedd could not suffer the laws and injustice of the French, they rose up a second time in opposition to them, with Owain ab Edwin, who had before brought the French to Anglesey, as their leader. (Pen.20[1]21).

L.17. Cadugavn: Cadwgan ap Bleddyn, who ruled in Ceredigion and Powys, including Meirionnydd. He clearly created an impression on his contemporaries, as may be gathered from the many references to him in the Brut. He opposed Rhys ap Tewdwr in 1088 and played a leading part in the revolt of 1094, and in 1096. He fled to Ireland with Gruffudd ap Cynan in 1098, and the following year returned and took possession of Ceredigion and part of Powys. It is clear that he was an unstable character, and more than once fell out of favour with the king. He was killed through treachery in 1111.

His restless son Owain caused him no end of trouble. It was Owain who abducted Nest, his cousin and daughter of Rhys ap Tewdwr, who was married to the Norman, Gerald de Windsor, c.1100. **Ls.17-18. Maredud y vravt.** He also is given much attention in the Brut, and his life was certainly not without incident. When the king campaigned against him in 1121, he was refused refuge in Gwynedd, and obliged to pay a heavy fine to the king. He continued to encounter difficulties and problems until his death in 1131, when he is described by the Brut as 'the splendour and defence of the men of Powys.' He 'died after having done penance on his soul and body and worthily receiving the Body of Christ;' cf. Pen. 20[1] 50.

P.45. **L.3. y daw** 'his son-in-law.' Gruffudd's daughter Gwenllian had been married to Cadwgan; she was the mother of his son Madog. But Cadwgan had other wives *(RB 99, 101)*; one of them was a Norman, daughter of Picot de Sai (Ibid. 63, 101). **L.14. Iddewon.** Note the way in which the aggressive Normans are described as Jews. **Ls.18-19. yr yeirll ... ag eu hemlynassant wynteu** 'the earls pursued them.' In the Brut it is said that the Welsh were killed on the island. The

Normans came to Anglesey, after Gruffudd and Cadwgan had retreated to Ireland: 'And after the French had come into the island, they slew many of the island,' Pen.20[1] 21.

L.23. trwy weledigaeth Duw. The author of the *Historia* is the only one who places this interpretation on the appearance of the fleet.

.46. **L.5. brenhin Llychlyn:** Magnus Barefoot, king of Norway, son of Olaf Haraldsson. c.1093-1103 were the years of his reign.

Ls.5-6. a gyvarwyddassei Duw. 'whom God had directed.' No one else suggests it was God who directed Magnus towards Anglesey. According to the Brut he 'approached the island of Anglesey, and a fleet with him, thinking to conquer all the island of Britain' (Pen.20[1] 21).

L.33. Fferyll: Virgil. A reference to the *Eclogues* i.63: *et penitus toto divisos orbe Brittanos.*

.47. **P.28. yn y kantref hwnnw.** The *cantref* is not named, although it is fair to suggest that Rhos is meant, the cantref to the east of the Conway. Cf. the Brut (s.a. 1099). After Cadwgan ap Bleddyn and Gruffudd ap Cynan had returned from Ireland, and peace had been made with the Normans, 'Cadwgan ap Bleddyn received a portion of Powys and Ceredigion, and Gruffudd ap Cynan received Anglesey' (Pen.20[1] 21).

L.29. eu vuchedd 'his life.' *eu* is the form of the 3 pl. of the possessive pronoun, but the 3 sing. is required here.

.48. **L.1. Henri, vrenhin Lloegyr:** Henry I, who was on the throne from 1100 till his death in 1135, son of the Conqueror and brother of William Rufus, who was killed in 1100. Gruffudd must have visited him in 1100 or some time later, if

NOTES (page 48)

the account we have here is correct. Apparently, it took place during the time Hervé was bishop of Bangor, and before 1109, when he was translated to Ely.

Ls.4–5. Erfyn, eskob Bangor. This is Hervé, the Breton who was made bishop of Bangor by the Normans in 1092. He belonged to the court of William Rufus, and was in favour with the king. Not so with the Welsh in Bangor, however, and after some years it appears that he was driven out. It is not impossible that he served as a mediator between Gruffudd and the king, although there is no evidence of this anywhere else. He was clearly a man of importance, as is testified by the frequent references to him in various chronicles. In 1109 there was established the diocese of Ely, and Hervé was consecrated as its first bishop.

The situation in Bangor must have been dismal and desperate at this time, with little evidence of the prosperity which seems to have come later. Cf.49–50 below. The see remained vacant until 1120 when David was appointed bishop. There is a tradition that Urban, bishop of Llandaf, was in charge during this period, which may explain why he succeeded in organizing the removal to Llandaf of Dubricius's remains from Bardsey in 1120.

L.7. Arllechwedd: the cantref between Arfon and Rhos, and to the west of the river Conway.
Ls.18–19. heb gannyat yarll Kaer 'without the permission of the earl of Chester.' It appears that Hugh, earl of Chester, was still in possession of Rhos, even after the unsuccessful expedition of 1098, but there is the suggestion that he was beginning to lose his grip. Hugh died in 1101. It

is, of course, possible that his son, Richard, is the one meant here; he was only seven years of age when his father died.

L.28. megis am wlat yr Israel... In 605 BC Jehoiakim, king of Judah, was defeated by Nebuchadnezzar, king of Babylon. Jerusalem fell in 587, and the inhabitants taken captive to Babylon. There they remained until they were freed by Cyrus, king of Persia, in 539.

L.30. yr yarll, doubtless the earl of Chester, Richard son of Hugh referred to above. According to the Brut he was one of the leaders of the forces which came to Wales in 1114, and was one of those who had complained to the king about the behaviour of the Welsh: 'And in the meantime also the son of Hugh, earl of Chester, had accused Gruffudd ap Cynan and Goronwy ab Owain' (Pen. 20[1] 37).

Ls.34-35. dwyn ganthaw vrenhin Yskotlont... a gwyr y Deheu. This must refer to the expedition of 1114. The *Historia* gives the impression that it was aimed against Gruffudd and Gwynedd, but the Brut mentions Powys also: 'A year after that, Henry, king of England moved a host against the men of Gwynedd, and above all to Powys' (Pen. 20[1] 37). The king had mustered three hosts: 'In the meantime, the king got together three hosts: one from Cornwall and Deheubarth and French and Saxons from Dyfed, with Gilbert fitz Richard as their leader, and another host from the North and Scotland with two leaders over them, namely Alexander, son of Maelcoluim, and the son of Hugh, earl of Chester, and the third host along with himself' (ibid).

P.49. L.2. Mur Castell: Tomen y Mur in Ardudwy, not

far from Trawsfynydd. It contained an old Roman fort, within which a castle had been built later. It was clearly a place of strategic importance at one time as well as being a political centre. According to the *Historia* (43.17), William Rufus was there, but there is no evidence of this in any other source. Certainly a road led thither from England. Cf. e.g. J. Beeler: 'Farther south, another route into Wales is said to have followed the course of a Roman road from Oswestry across the Berwyn range to the valley of the Dee, and thence by way of the valleys of Afon Trywryn and Afon Prysor to Mur Castell in the vicinity of Trawsfynydd. The latter part is certainly Roman, but there is doubt about the section from Oswestry to the Dee valley,' *Warfare in England 1066-1189* (New York, 1966), p.194. Further Nash-Williams *(RFW* 112): 'This fort... lies at the point where the road from Caernarvon and Llystyn to Caer Gai crossed the road running south from Caerhun to Pennal.' The site reveals three main periods of occupation, the latest being represented by a Norman motte. (Cf. Ibid).

Ls.4-6. **Ag oddyno ymanfon a'r brenhin... a thangnefeddu.** The account in the Brut is different and more detailed. On the initiative of Owain ap Cadwgan (who is not mentioned here), the Welsh princes formed an alliance to resist the enemy. But this alliance was broken because the king and his men sought to negotiate separately with the princes. Gruffudd was the last and got the least favourable terms: 'And the king took him into his peace upon his paying him a large tribute;' cf. Pen. 20[1] 37-38.

Ls.8-9. **eilweith... y doeth Henri vrenhin.** There

is doubtless here a reference to Henry's expedition of 1121, which is recorded in the Brut
and in other works; cf. Pen. 20[1] 47-48, where
the account of the expedition and the part played
by Gruffudd is so different from the impression
given by the *Historia:* 'the king moved a mighty
host against the men of Powys, where Maredudd
ap Bleddyn and the sons of Cadwgan ap Bleddyn,
Einon and Madog and Morgan, were lords. And
when they heard that, they sent messengers to
Gruffudd ap Cynan, who held the island of
Anglesey, to ask him whether he would unite
with them against the king... but he had made
peace with the king, and he informed them that,
if they fled, near his bounds, he would come
against them and would despoil them.'
**Ls.20-21. y kerddws drachefyn gan wneuthur
tangnefedd ag ef.** The king returned, having made
peace with Gruffudd. Not so the Brut, however,
where there is no mention of Gruffudd in connection with the peace. The names mentioned
are those of Maredudd ap Bleddyn and the sons
of Cadwgan: 'And Maredudd and the sons of
Cadwgan came to his peace. And after they had
made peace with the king, the king returned to
England after imposing a heavy tribute of animals
upon Maredudd and the sons of Cadwgan - about
ten thousand head.' (Pen. 20[1] 48).
.50. L.2. eglwysseu 'churches.' Likewise in the Brut
in the notice of his death, 'after building many
churches and consecrating them to God and the
saints' (Pen. 20[1] 52). This also characterized
the reign of Brian Ború in Ireland at the beginning
of the eleventh century (cf. *CGRG* 138-40), and
that of Eystein in Norway at the beginning of

the twelfth (cf. *H* 699). Further, we may mention David I of Scotland: 'David I, the maker of Scotland,... after 1124 sole king over the whole of Scotland... He was Scotland's great church reformer... In the years between 1125 and 1150 there were founded and built no less than seven cathedrals in addition to a number of smaller churches and abbeys.' (*AE* 157).

Ls.3-4. perllanneu a garddeu. Note the evidence of Gerald: 'They [the Welsh] do not have orchards or gardens, but if you give them fruit or garden produce they are only too pleased to eat it' (*GW* 252).

L.8. adeiladoedd. This is difficult to explain as it stands. A verb seems to be required here, which originally may have taken the form *deliis/ de[l]lis* (3 sing. pret. of *dal[y]* 'hold' in Middle Welsh). Then *-oedd* could have been added after *-s*, anticipating *-oedd* in *lyssoedd. deliis* etc. had become unfamiliar, and an obscure form could have been emended to *adeiladoedd* 'buildings,' a form which would be understood, though not appropriate here, where we should read *a deliis* 'he held (courts, feasts').

L.9. gwleddeu. One wonders whether there is a reference here to festivals or eisteddfods held by Gruffudd for poets and minstrels. The tradition associating his name with a revival and revision of the bardic craft is well-known. *Gwled* is the name given by the Brut to the eisteddfod held in Cardigan by Rhys ap Gruffudd in 1176; cf. *RB* 166.

Ls.14-15. A'e feibeon... ar y kantrefoedd eithaf idav. Cf. the accounts of the expeditions of the sons of Gruffudd against the territories bordering

on Gwynedd, and the way in which the confines
of the kingdom were extended eastwards beyond
the Conway to Rhos, Rhufoniog and Dyffryn
Clwyd, and southwards towards Meirionnydd, an
expansion achieved mainly at the expense of
Powys; cf. *RB* 109-17.

Ls.19-20. A'r brenhinoedd bychein ereill. The
author must have been thinking of chieftains who
had been in difficulties, such as Gruffudd ap Rhys
in 1115 *(RB* 82), Maredudd ap Bleddyn and the
sons of Cadwgan ap Bleddyn in 1121 *(Ibid,* 104),
and Maredudd ap Cadwgan in 1124 *(Ibid,* 108).
But Gruffudd was not so forthcoming with his
help and support as the *Historia* suggests.

L.28. y ddwyn buchedd ddwywawl. It was by no
means unusual for a secular leader to assume the
habit of a monk at the end of his days. Cf. D.
Knowles, *The Monastic Order in England* (Cam-
bridge, 1949, 635-6.

Ls.32-33. y brenhin Ezechias: Hezekiah, king of
Judah; see 2 Kings xviii-xx, 2 Chron. xxix-xxxii,
Is. xxxvi-xxxix. 'And he did that which was right
in the sight of the Lord, according to all that
David his father did,' 2 Kings xviii.3.

The king is warned about his death, and the
prophet Isaiah tells him, 'Set thine house in order:
for thou shalt die, and not live' (Is. xxxviii. 1).
But after praying and weeping, he is promised
fifteen more years; the comparison with Hezekiah
is therefore not quite appropriate. Yet Hezekiah
was a king with much wealth and treasures, 2.
Chron. xxxii. 27-29, Is. xxxix.2.

L.35. swllt. Here it appears to denote a definite
sum of money, but it is not possible to determine
how much. It comes from the Latin *sol'dus*

solidus, and at an early period meant 'treasure, wealth.'

Ls.35-51.1. eglwys **Grist:** Christ Church, founded by king Sitric c.1030, after he had returned to Dublin from Rome.

P.51. L.3. eglwys **Fynyw:** St David's.

L.4. manachlog **Gaer.** Some institution existed there from an early period, but it was in 1093 that Hugh earl of Chester founded a monastery there. The first abbot was Richard, a monk from Bec; see *OV* iii.286.

Ls.4-5. manachlog **Amwythig.** It was founded by Roger, earl of Shrewsbury, in 1083, and his son Hugh was buried there. The father of the historian Ordericus Vitalis played a part in its foundation, and became a member of it. Ordericus himself was brought up there until he left, at the age of ten.

L.5. eglwys **Vangor,** Bangor in Arfon, the church whose foundation is connected with the name of Deiniol, a saint from the sixth century.

The list which follows appears to represent the more important churches in north Wales.

L.6. **Caergybi:** Holyhead, a church connected with the name of Cybi, a saint of the sixth century. This church and the one in Penmon were the most renowned in Anglesey, and by the time of Gruffudd had centuries of history behind them. **Penmon,** in the south-east of Anglesey. Opposite is Ynys Lannog (Ynys Seiriol), where the saints settled at an early period. The founding of the settlement in Penmon is connected with Seiriol, a saint of the sixth century. Like Bardsey, Penmon in the twelfth century became an Augustinian settlement.

L.7. Celynnawg: Clynnog Fawr in Arfon, on the northern coast of the Llŷn peninsula between Caernarfon and Nefyn. The founding of the settlement is connected with Beuno, another sixth century saint. It appears that for a while in the thirteenth century the regulars there adopted the Cistercian order.

Enlli: The settlement on Bardsey, the island opposite Aberdaron on the tip of the Llŷn peninsula. To Bardsey the saints retired to rest, and we are told that twenty thousand of them lay buried there; cf. *LL* 1-2. It is impossible to determine how early the settlement was.

L.8. Meifod: a church of Tysilio, a Powys saint again from the sixth century, son of Brochfael Ysgithrog and brother of Cynan Garwyn, whose praises were sung by the poet Taliesin in a poem which may well be the earliest in the language. It was near to Mathrafael, the political centre of Powys, and was one of the main churches.

Llan Armawn: the church of Garmon, probably the fifth century saint Germanus of Auxerre, who visited Britain twice in the fifth century. His name is borne by many churches in Powys. Llanarmon-yn-lâl is probably meant here.

L.9. Dineirth: Dinerth or Llandrillo-yn-Rhos, an important ecclesiastical site.

L.16. Dafydd eskob Bangor. He was consecrated in 1120, and was in Bangor, at least until 1137, when Gruffudd died. His successor Meurig was appointed in 1139. He seems to have been quite active and resourceful, judging by the references to him in various sources.

L.17. Symeon archdiagon. According to the Brut he died in 1152. He must have been a man of

influence in Gwynedd, and in the Brut he is described as 'a man of great authority and dignity'
(Pen. 20[1] 58). He may have been behind some
of the policies of Owain and Cadwaladr, such as
their support for Bernard, bishop of St. David's.
Bernard sent him a letter (1147/8) asking him to
support the campaign for metropolitan status,
and to offer evidence before the Pope. So Gerald
tells us; see *EAWD* i.2654, and cf. *ibid* 101,
198-9.

L.20. herwydd gorchymyn Yago ebostol: 'Is any
sick among you? let him call for the elders of
the church; and let him pray over him, anointing
him with oil in the name of the Lord.' James V.14.

L.23. Yago padriarch: Jacob; see Gen. xlix.

L.27. yn y ddiwedd ddyddyeu. Apparently *yny
ddyddyeu* 'in his days' should be read here.

P.52. **Ls.1-2.** Ioswe, fab Nwn: Joshua, who was chosen
to lead the Hebrews after the death of Moses,
and who brought the people to Canaan; a wise,
strong, religious, selfless man. Before he dies,
he urges the people to be faithful to God, and
renews the covenant between them (Joshua xxiii-
xxiv), and then, 'And it came to pass after these
things, that Joshua, the son of Nun, the servant
of the Lord, died, being an hundred and ten years
old.' (xxiv.29). But there is no mention of the
grief of the people.

L.3. yna y bu farw. There is a record of his
death in the Brut s.a.1137, accompanied by a not
ungrateful appreciation of his life and works:

> In that year Gruffudd ap Cynan, prince of
> Gwynedd and head and king and defender and
> pacifier of all Wales, ended his temporal life
> in Christ, and died after many perils by sea

132

and land and after innumerable victories in
wars and the winning of spoils, after great
wealth of gold and silver, after gathering the
men of Gwynedd together from the several
lands whither the Normans had dispersed
them, after building many churches and consecrating them to God and the saints - after
receiving extreme unction and communion
and confession and repentance for his sins,
and becoming a monk and making a good end
in his perfect old age. (Pen. 20[1] 52).

L.4. yn y parth assw y'r allawr fawr. Cf. Ralegh
Radford: 'This proves that the east end at least
was completed by this date and it seems possible
that Gruffudd ap Cynan was claiming burial by
the altar as founder of the building. The ca-
thedral may therefore be dated to the second
quarter of the twelfth century, a period in full
accord with the character of the remains' (AC c
[1949],258].

ABBREVIATIONS
Bibliographical

AC   *Archaeologia Cambrensis*

AE   A. W. Brøgger, *Ancient Emigrants. A History of the Norse Settlements of Scotland* (Oxford, 1929)

B   *The Bulletin of the Board of Celtic Studies*

BD   H. Lewis, *Brut Dingestow* (Caerdydd, 1942)

BT   J. G. Evans, *The Book of Taliesin* (Llanbedrog, 1910)

CGRG   J. H. Todd, *Cogadh Gaedhel re Gallaibh. The War of the Gaedhil and the Gaill* (R. S., London, 1867)

CR   Dillon & Chadwick, *Celtic Realms* (London, 1967)

EAWD   J. C. Davies, *Episcopal Acts and Cognate Documents relating to Welsh Dioceses, 1066-1272* 2 vols. (Hist. Soc. Church in Wales Pubns., Cardiff, 1948 & 1953)

EWGT   P. C. Bartrum, *Early Welsh Genealogical Tracts* (Cardiff, 1966)

GW   L. Thorpe (trans.), *Gerald of Wales: The Journey through Wales / The Description of Wales* (Penguin Books, 1978)

H   L. M. Hollander, *Heimskringla, History of the Kings of Norway* by Snorri Sturluson (Univ of Texas Press, Austin, 1964)

HB   *Historia Brittonum* (early ninth Century)

HGVK   D. S. Evans, *Historia Gruffud Vab Kenan* (Caerdydd, 1977)

HV   T. D. Kendrick, *A History of the Vikings* (London, 1930, 1970)

HVW   Lewys Dwnn, *Heraldic Visitations of Wales* 2 vols. Ed. S. R. Meyrick (Llandovery, 1846)

HW   J. E. Lloyd, *A History of Wales from the Earliest Times to the Edwardian Conquest* 2 vols. (London, 1911)

LHDd   M. Richards, *The Laws of Hywel Dda* (Liverpool, 1954)

LHEB K. H. Jackson, *Language and History in early Britain* (Edinburgh, 1953)

LL J. Rhys & J. G. Evans, *Liber Landavensis* (Oxford, 1893)

LIB S. J. Williams & J. E. Powell, *Cyfreithiau Hywel Dda yn ôl Llyfr Blegywryd* (Caerdydd, 1942)

ONRW B. G. Charles, *Old Norse Relations with Wales* (Cardiff, 1934)

OV Ordericus Vitalis (1075-1143), *Historiae Ecclesiasticae*

Pen. A Peniarth Manuscript in the National Library of Wales.

Pen.20.[1] *Brut y Tywysogyon or the Chronicle of the Princes Peniarth MS. Version.* trans. T Jones (Cardiff, 1952)

RB *Brut y Tywysogyon or the Chronicle of the Princes Red Book of Hergest Version* Ed. and trans. T. Jones (Cardiff, 1955)

RC *Revue celtique*

RFW V. E. Nash-Williams, *The Roman Frontier in Wales* 2nd. ed. M. G. Jarrett (Cardiff, 1969)

TC *Transactions of the Honourable Society of Cymmrodorion*

TWTP J. Rhys, *Tours in Wales by Thomas Pennant, Esq.*, 3 vols. (Caernarvon, 1883)

TYP R. Bromwich, *Trioedd Ynys Prydein* (Cardiff, 1961)

VSBG A. W. Wade-Evans, *Vitae Sanctorum Britanniae et Genealogiae* (Cardiff, 1944)

WAL R. S. Loomis, *Wales and the Arthurian Legend* (Cardiff, 1956)

WHR *Welsh History Review*

WLW D. Jenkins & M. E. Owen, *The Welsh Law of Women* (Cardiff, 1980)

WM J. G. Evans, *The White Book Mabinogion* (Pwllheli, 1907); reprint with new introduction by R. M. Jones (Caerdydd, 1973).

INDEX

The forms listed here are such as are referred to in the notes. They consist of ordinary words, names of persons/people, and names of places.

Words

adeiladoedd 50.8

albryswyr 35.30

amravaellyon yeithyoed 39.2

barwn 38.7

baut deheu 38.22-23

buchedd 47.29, 50.29

bwyeill deuvinyauc 36.23

cantref 47.28, -oedd 50.15

castell 39.8, c. y Freinc 41.2

castellwyr 44.7

kenveint 38.27

clas 35.11

kyvranc 32.37

daleassant 38.19

daw 45.3

deudec prif emlad 33.16

deudeng blyned 38.21-22

dieither 38.16

dieuoed 38.4

dyledawc 33.7

dywededigyon 36.14

eglwysseu 50.2

escob 35.10

garddeu 50.4

gleiuyauc 36.25

gwleddeu 50.9

y ddiwedd ddyddyeu 51.27

mudav 33.35

nodua 35.21

peleu haearnaul kyllellauc 34.24

perllanneu 50.3

porth 35.2

priodolder 38.2

swllt 50.37

teir llong 42.9

triugein llong 40.35

trwydet 35.1

uchof 36.14

y parth assw y'r allawr fawr 52.4

Names of persons/people

Angharat 42.27

Antiochus 44.5

Arthur 33.14

brenhin Llychlyn 46.5

brenhin Yskotlont 48.34-35

brenhinoedd bychein 50.19

Catwalader 43.2-3

Catwallavn 43.2

Cadugavn 44.17

Caradauc m. Gruffud 35.28

Custennin amperauder 39.9

Kendelu m. Conus 36.8-9

Dafydd eskob Bangor 51.16

Dauyd vrenhin 41.9-10, 44.2

Demetrius 33.8

Diermit 35.1

Duw 45.23, 46.6

Erfyn, eskob Bangor 48.4-5

Ysai 40.16

Ewein 43.2

Ewein vab Edwin 42.27, 44.13

Fferyll 46.33

Fichtyeit 33.17

Freinc 44.1

Gellan telynyaur penkerd 42.16
Gollwyn 40.10
Gothrei vrenhin 40.29
Guallter yarll Henford 34.18
Gvarin o Amwythic 34.18
Gvenhvyssyon 35.29
Guenlliant 43.3
Gwyndit 36.8
gwyr y Deheu 48.35
Henri, vrenhin (Lloegyr)
    48.1, 49.8-9
Hu arall 44.8-9
Hu yarll 38.5
Hu yarll Amvythic 38.10
Yago ebostol 51.20
Yago padriarch 51.23
yarll Kaer 48.18-19
Idewon 45.14
Ioswe, fab Nwn 52.1-2
Maredud 44.17
Maro vard 42.23
Meilir m. Riwallaun 35.31
Meiryaun Goch 16.28
Nordmannyeit 35.30
Royzer 38.10
Rys m. Teudur 35.9
Symeon archdiagon 51.17
Tullius vard 42.23
Ulkessar 33.11
y brenhin Ezechias 50.32-33
yr yarll 48.30
yr yeirll 45.18

Names of places
Aberdaron 40.22
archescopty Mynyv 35.8
Arvon 39.9, 41.19

Arllechwedd 48.7
Bronn yr Erv 31.1
Cabidyldy Ruvein 33.14
Caergybi 51.6
Caer Lwytcoet 34.18-19
Castell Baldwin 38.11
Celynnawg 51.7
Deheubarth Kemry 35.10
Dineirth 51.9
Dyfrynt Cluyt 41.20
Edeirnyavn 38.13
eglwys Vangor 51.5
eglwys Fynyw 51.3
eglwys Grist 50.35-51.1
Eiuyonyd ac Arduduy 41.19
Enlli 51.7
Gwent Uch Coet/Is Coet
    35.28-29
gwlat yr Israel 48.28
Gwyned 43.10
Llan Armawn 51.8
Lleyn 42.19
Llwch Garmavn 32.36
manachlog Amwythig 51.4-5
manachlog Gaer 51.4
Meifod 51.8
Morgannvc 35.29-30
Mur Castell 43.17, 49.2
Menyd Carn 37.27
Mynyv 35.8
Penmon 51.6
Porth Cleis 35.7
Porth Hodni 39.32
Porthlarc 35.3
porth Nevyn 41.17
Ros 41.20
y Ruc 38.12

Also published by
Llanerch:

TALIESIN POEMS
translated by
Meirion Pennar.

THE BLACK BOOK
OF CARMARTHEN
with translations by
Meirion Pennar.

WISDOM OF THE
DAOIST MASTERS
by Leon Weiger.

NORTHUMBRIAN CROSSES
by W. G. Collingwood.

For a complete list,
write to:
Llanerch Enterprises,
Felinfach, Lampeter,
Dyfed SA48 8PJ.